The Music Man

THE MUSIC MAN

Book, Music and Lyrics by

MEREDITH WILLSON

Story by Meredith Willson
and Franklin Lacey

G. P. Putnam's Sons   New York

© 1958 by Meredith Willson

Library of Congress Catalog

Card Number: 58-8901

Third Impression

MANUFACTURED IN THE UNITED STATES OF AMERICA

43924   VAN REES PRESS • NEW YORK

To My Rini

Author's Preface

The brilliance of Morton Da Costa's staging and direction of *The Music Man* has been observed and praised by many. I should like to say that Mr. Da Costa's genius also includes playwriting and editing of the highest order, which talents he exercised unstintingly in the creative collaboration that brought *The Music Man* to life.

The Music Man produced by Kermit Bloomgarden with Herbert Greene in association with Frank Productions, Inc., opened at the Majestic Theatre, New York City on December 19, 1957 with the following cast:

CAST

(In order of appearance)

TRAVELLING SALESMEN .... *Russell Goodwin, Hal Norman, Robert Howard, James Gannon, Robert Lenn, Vernon Lusby, Robert Evans*

CHARLIE COWELL .... *Paul Reed*
CONDUCTOR .... *Carl Nicholas*
HAROLD HILL .... *Robert Preston*
MAYOR SHINN .... *David Burns*
EWART DUNLOP .... *Al Shea* ⎫ **THE**
OLIVER HIX .... *Wayne Ward* ⎬ **BUFFALO**
JACEY SQUIRES .... *Vern Reed* ⎮ **BILLS**
OLIN BRITT .... *Bill Spangenberg* ⎭
MARCELLUS WASHBURN .... *Iggie Wolfington*
TOMMY DJILAS .... *Danny Carroll*
MARIAN PAROO .... *Barbara Cook*
MRS. PAROO .... *Pert Kelton*
AMARYLLIS .... *Marilyn Siegel*
WINTHROP PAROO .... *Eddie Hodges*
EULALIE MACKECKNIE SHINN ...... *Helen Raymond*
ZANEETA SHINN .... *Dusty Worrall*
GRACIE SHINN .... *Barbara Travis*
ALMA HIX .... *Adnia Rice*
MAUD DUNLOP .... *Elaine Swann*
ETHEL TOFFELMIER .... *Peggy Mondo*
MRS. SQUIRES .... *Martha Flynn*
CONSTABLE LOCKE .... *Carl Nicholas*

9

RIVER CITY TOWNSPEOPLE AND KIDS

Pamela Abbott, Babs Delmore, Martha Flynn, Janet Hayes, Peggy Mondo, Barbara Williams, Elaine Swann, Marie Santella, Marlys Watters, James Gannon, Russell Goodwin, Robert Howard, Peter Leeds, Robert Lenn, Hal Norman, Carl Nicholas, Joan Bowman, Alice Clift, Nancy Davis, Penny Ann Green, Lynda Lynch, Jacqueline Maria, Marilyn Poudrier, Pat Mariano, Elisabeth Buda, Babs Warden, Tom Panko, Ronn Cummins, Robert Evans, Vernon Lusby, Gary Menteer, John Sharpe, Roy Wilson, Gerald Teijelo, Bob Mariano, Vernon Wendorf.

The Music Man was directed by Morton Da Costa

Choreography by Onna White

Settings and Lighting by Howard Bay

Costumes by Raoul Pene Du Bois

Musical Direction and Vocal Arrangements by Herbert Greene

Orchestration by Don Walker and Sidney Fine

Dance Arrangements by Laurence Rosenthal

Musical Synopsis of Scenes

ACT I.

Scene 1. A Railway Coach. Morning, July 4, 1912.

ROCK ISLAND ... *Charlie Cowell & Travelling Salesmen*

Scene 2. River City, Iowa. Center of Town. Immediately following.

IOWA STUBBORN .... *Townspeople of River City*
TROUBLE .... *Harold and Townspeople*

Scene 3. The Paroos' House. That evening.

PIANO LESSON .... *Marian, Mrs. Paroo, Amaryllis*
GOODNIGHT MY SOMEONE .... *Marian*

Scene 4. Madison Gymnasium Thirty minutes later.

SEVENTY SIX TROMBONES .. *Harold, Boys and Girls*
SINCERE .... *Olin, Oliver, Ewart, Jacey*

Scene 5. Exterior of Madison Library. Immediately following.

THE SADDER-BUT-WISER GIRL .... *Harold and*
Marcellus
PICKALITTLE .. *Eulalie, Maud, Ethel, Alma, Mrs. Squires,*
Ladies of River City
GOODNIGHT LADIES ..... *Olin, Oliver, Ewart, Jacey*

Scene 6. Interior of Madison Library. Immediately following.

MARIAN THE LIBRARIAN .... *Harold, Boys and Girls*

Scene 7. A Street. The following Saturday noon.

Scene 8. The Paroos' Porch. That evening.

MY WHITE KNIGHT .... *Marian*

Scene 9. Center of Town. Noon, the following Saturday.

WELLS FARGO WAGON .... *Winthrop and*
Townspeople

ACT II.

Scene 1. Madison Gymnasium. The following Tuesday evening.

IT'S YOU .... *Olin, Oliver, Ewart, Jacey, Eulalie, Maud, Ethel, Alma and Mrs. Squires*

SHIPOOPI .... *Marcellus, Harold, Marian, Tommy, Zaneeta, and Kids*

PICKALITTLE REPRISE .... *Eulalie, Maud, Ethel, Alma, Mrs. Squires and Ladies*

Scene 2. The Hotel Porch. The following Wednesday evening.

LIDA ROSE .... *Olin, Oliver, Ewart, Jacey*

WILL I EVER TELL YOU .... *Marian*

Scene 3. The Paroos' Porch. Immediately following.

GARY, INDIANA .... *Winthrop*

Scene 4. The Footbridge. Fifteen minutes later.

IT'S YOU REPRISE ...... *Townspeople, Boys and Girls*

TILL THERE WAS YOU .... *Marian and Harold*

Scene 5. A Street. Immediately following.

SEVENTY SIX TROMBONES and GOODNIGHT MY SOMEONE .... *Harold and Marian*

Scene 6. Madison Park. A few minutes later.

TILL THERE WAS YOU REPRISE . ... *Harold*

Scene 7. River City High School Assembly Room. Immediately following.

FINALE .... *Entire Company*

12

ACT ONE

Scene 1

TIME: *The morning of July 4th, 1912*

PLACE: *On a train somewhere in Iowa*

AT RISE: *Train effect scrim rises on a red-plushed, kerosene-lamped, enamel-drinking-cupped railway coach in full cry. One seat has been turned in the coach to accommodate a card game—the participants being three travelling salesmen and a stranger whose back is to the audience and who is concentrated throughout the scene on winning every pot, which he drops by handfuls into an open suitcase on the floor by his side. A fourth salesman is kibitzing. A few seats forward in the coach a fifth salesman is reading a newspaper, until he finds himself drawn into the conversation among the salesmen. Several other passengers are behind newspapers. We hear "train-slowing-down" music. The train slows and stops.*

CONDUCTOR

(*Poking head into Coach L*)

River City Junction—River City next station stop!

(*He exits*)

SALESMAN #1

You're crazy with the heat. Credit is no good for a notion salesman.

CONDUCTOR
(Poking head into coach again)
Boart! All aboart!
(Exits)

SALESMAN #2
Why not? What's the matter with credit?

SALESMAN #1
It's old-fashioned. Charlie, you're an anvil salesman. Your firm give credit?
(Train makes starting noise in orchestra)

CHARLIE
No sir!

SALESMAN #1
Nor anybody else.
(Train starting)

CONDUCTOR
River City, River City next.

SALESMAN #1
Cash for the merchandise—*cash* for the button-hooks—

SALESMAN #3
(Nodding)
Cash for the cotton goods—cash for the hard goods—**cash** for the soft goods—

SALESMAN #1
Cash for the fancy goods—

SALESMAN #2

Cash for the noggins and the piggins and the firkins.

SALESMAN #3

Cash for the hogshead, cask and demijohn. Cash for the crackers, and the pickles and the *fly*-paper.

SALESMAN #4
(Train at running speed)
Look whadayatalk, whadayatalk, whadayatalk, whadayatalk, whadayatalk?

SALESMAN #5

Wheredayagitit?

SALESMAN #4

Whadayatalk?

SALESMAN #1

Ya can talk, ya can talk, ya can bicker, ya can talk, ya can bicker bicker bicker, ya can talk, ya can talk, ya can talk, talk, talk, talk, bicker, bicker, bicker, you can talk all ya wanna but it's differnt than it was.

CHARLIE

(Ill-tempered)
No it ain't, no it ain't, but ya gotta know the territory.

SALESMAN #3
Chi chi chi chi chi chi chi. Why it's the Model T Ford made the trouble, made the people want to go wanna git wanna git wanna git up and go 7,8,9,10,12,14,22,23 miles to the county seat—

SALESMAN #1

Yes sir Yes sir.

SALESMAN #3

Who's gonna patronize a little bitty *two-by-four* kinda store anymore?
> (*As each newspaper reader speaks* HE *lowers his paper long enough for his line, then it goes back up before his face*)

SALESMAN #4

Whatdayatalk, whatdayatalk.

SALESMAN #5

Wheredyagitit.

CHARLIE

Not the Model T at all, take a gander at the store, at the *Mod*ren store, at the present day store at the present day modren departmentalized groc'ry store.

SALESMAN #4

Whadayatalk, whadayatalk, whadayatalk, whadayatalk, whadayatalk.

SALESMAN #5

Wheredayagitit.

SALESMAN #4

Whadayatalk, whadayatalk, whadayatalk.

SALESMAN #5

Wheredayagitit.

SALESMAN #1

Ya can talk, ya can bicker, ya can talk, ya can bicker, ya can talk, talk, talk, talk, bicker, bicker, bicker, ya can talk all ya wanna but it's differnt than it was.

CHARLIE

No it ain't, but ya gotta know the territory.

SALESMAN #3

Why, it's the *U*needa Biscuit made the trouble *U*-needa, *U*-needa, put the crackers in a package, in a package the *U*-needa Biscuit in an air-tight sanitary package made the cracker barrel obsolete, obsolete.

CHARLIE

Obsolete, obsolete, obsolete.

SALESMAN #4

Cracker barrel went out the window with the Mail Pouch cut plug chawin' by the stove ... *changed* the approach of a travelin' salesman made it pretty hard—

CHARLIE

No it didn't no it didn't, but ya gotta know the territory.

SALESMAN #3

Gone, gone.

SALESMAN #1

Gone with the hogshead, cask and demijohn, gone with the sugar barrel, pickle barrel, milk pan, gone with the tub and the pail and the tierce.

SALESMAN #2

Ever meet a fellow by the *name a' Hill?*

SALESMAN #1

Hill?

CHARLIE

Hill!

SALESMAN #3

Hill?

SALESMAN #4

Hill?

NEWSPAPER #1

Hill?

NEWSPAPER #2

Hill?

SALESMAN #5

Hill?

SALESMAN #2

Hill!

ALL BUT CHARLIE

No!

(ALL NEWSPAPERS *go back up*)

CHARLIE

Just a minute, just a minute, just a minute—

SALESMAN #4

Never heard a' any *salesman* Hill—

SALESMAN #2

Now, he doesn't know the territory—

SALESMAN #1

Doesn't know the territory?

SALESMAN #3

What's the fella's line?

SALESMAN #2

Never worries 'bout his line.

SALESMAN #1

Never worries 'bout his line?

SALESMAN #2

Or the cracker barrel bein' obsolete, or the Uneeda Biscuit in an air-tight sanitary package or the Model T Ford—

CHARLIE

Just a minute, just a minute, just a minute—

SALESMAN #2

Never worries 'bout his line—

SALESMAN #3

Never worries 'bout his line.

SALESMAN #2

Or a doggone thing. *He's just a* bang beat bell-ringin' big haul, great go, neck-or-nothin' rip-roarin', ever'time-a-bull's-eye *sales*man, that's Professor Harold Hill.

SALESMAN #5

Tell us—what's his line? What's his line?

CHARLIE

He's a fake, and he doesn't know the terr—

SALESMAN #4

Whadayatalk, whadayatalk, whadayatalk, whadayatalk.

SALESMAN #2

He's a music man—

SALESMAN #3

He's a what? He's a what?

SALESMAN #2

He's a music man and he sells clarinets to the kids in the town with the big trombone and the ratatat drums and the big brass bass, big brass bass. And the piccolo the piccolo uniforms too with the shiny gold braid on the coat—and a big red stripe running—

SALESMAN #1

Welll—I don't know much about bands, but I do know you can't make a livin' sellin' big trombones or ratatat drums— No sir. Mandolin picks, perhaps, and here and there a jews-harp—

SALESMAN #2

No, the fella sells bands. *Boys Bands*. I don't know how he does it but he lives like a king, and he dallies and he gathers, and he plucks and he shines and when the man dances, certainly, boys, what else: the piper pays him. Yesss—sir.

Yes sir Yes sir Yes Sir. When the man dances, certainly boys, what else, the piper pays him.

ALL

Yes sir. Yes sir.

CHARLIE

But he doesn't know the territory!
(*Orchestra button. Train stops.*)

CONDUCTOR

(*Off*)
River City! River City!
(*Enters*)
River City! We're cross the state line into Iowa. River City! Population twenty two hundred and twelve. Seegarettes illegal in this state. Booart!
(*He exits*)

CHARLIE

All right, if you're all through I'll tell you about Harold Hill!

SALESMAN #2

You really know Harold Hill?

CHARLIE

Never saw him in my life but I know this much—he's giving every one of us a black eye! After he's worked a town over, the next salesman to arrive gets automatically tarred and feathered and rode out to the city limits on a rail.
(THEY *laugh*)
You think that's funny. Well, wait till it happens to you! Your hair *never grows back.*
(*He pulls off hat.* THEY *react*)

23

SALESMAN #1

But why should he get rode out'a town on a rail?

CHARLIE

Because in order to sell band instruments, *and* uniforms, *and* instruction books, he has to guarantee to teach the kids to play.

SALESMAN #3

Well?

CHARLIE

And to form them kids into a band! With himself as the leader!

SALESMAN #2

What's wrong with that?

CHARLIE

He don't know one note from another that's what's wrong with that! He can't tell a bass drum from a pipe organ! I'll catch up with that swindlin' two-bit thimble rigger, and when I do I'll squeal on him so loud—

SALESMAN #2

(*Laughing*)
Wow, you're mad, Charlie! Sure like to be around when you catch up with that fella.

CHARLIE

Well it won't be on this trip. Not in Iowa. Even the great Professor Hill wouldn't try to sell them neck-bowed Hawk-eyes out here.

ACT ONE   SCENE 1

CONDUCTOR

(*Off*)

Booaart!

(THE STRANGER *makes a fast decision, grabbing his winnings and suitcase*)

STRANGER

Gentlemen, you intrigue me. I think I'll have to give Iowa a try.

CHARLIE

(*Coldly*)

Don't believe I caught your name.

(STRANGER *turns and we see him for the first time. It is our hero.* HE *flashes suitcase which bears the legend* "PROF. HAROLD HILL" *and exits from train as all heads go out the windows. Coach splits in two to reveal a full stage view of River City's Main Street immediately following. The town is in 4th of July bunting and the stubborn Iowans are out in force.*)

Scene 2

TIME: *Immediately following*

AT RISE: River City, Iowa, center of town, exterior.
Townspeople are seen en tableau.
  (MAYOR SHINN *enters from the Billiard Parlor, leaving*
the door open for 2 WORKMEN *who enter carrying a*
large crate containing a visible pool table which they
take into the Billiard Parlor)

TOWNSPEOPLE
  (*Sing*)
Oh, there's nothing halfway about the Iowa way
    to treat you
When we treat you
Which we may not do at all.
There's an Iowa kind of special chip-on-the-shoul-
    der attitude
We've never been without
That we recall.
We can be cold as our falling thermometers in
    December
If you ask about our weather in July.
And we're so by God stubborn we can stand
    touchin' noses
For a week at a time and never see eye-to-eye.
But what the heck, you're welcome,
Join us at the picnic,

26

You can eat your fill of all the food you bring
>   yourself.
You really ought to give Iowa a try.
Provided you are contrary.

BOY

Good morning, Mayor Shinn.

MAN

Good morning, Mayor Shinn.

SHINN

It is, if you wanta go round in your drawers all day.
>   (*Music phrase*)

ALMA

And there I was in the Madison Hospital and nobody come
to see me. Cousin Will never come, Aunt Bertha never
come—

ETHEL

Your Aunt Bertha's dead.

ALMA

She wouldn't a'come anyway.

TOWNSPEOPLE
>   (*Sing*)
>   We can be cold as our falling thermometers in
>   December
>   If you ask about our weather in July
>   And we're so by God stubborn we can stand
>   touchin' noses

27

For a week at a time and never see eye-to-eye
    (*A capella à la chorale*)
But we'll give you our shirt
And a back to go with it
If your crops should happen to die
    (*The 2* WORKMEN *leave Billiard Parlor carry-*
    ing pool table packing case frame to center,
    as FARMER & WIFE *who have entered meet*
    down center. THEY *turn inside frame for*
    short pose as Grant Wood's "American
    Gothic.")

FARMER

(*Breaking pose to sing in tempo*)
So what the heck, you're welcome
Glad to have you with us

FARMER & WIFE

Even though we may not ever mention it again

TOWNSPEOPLE

You really ought to give Iowa
Hawkeye Iowa
Dubuque, Des Moines, Davenport, Marshalltown,
Mason City, Keokuk, Ames, Clear Lake
Ought to give Iowa a try.
    (HAROLD *crosses to business front labelled*
    "RIVER CITY LIVERY STABLE, JACEY SQUIRES,
    Prop." HAROLD *addresses a short, wiry man*
    about 36, JACEY SQUIRES)

HAROLD

Ah, Mr. Squires? Yes, I'm interested in a rig for Sunday,
if you could accommodate me.

JACEY

(*In a high-pitched tenor*)
Then I expect you'd ought to see the man in charge a'hirin rigs.

(*Exiting into Livery Stable, he turns*)
Who is late as usyal.

(MARCELLUS WASHBURN, *roundish, perspiring, enters hurriedly from the wings. At livery stable door he takes out his key. As he is about to open the door he looks up and sees* HAROLD, *rubs his eyes in disbelief*)

MARCELLUS

Hey, Gregory!

HAROLD

Marcellus!

MARCELLUS

You old son of a gun! What in—

HAROLD

(*Hastily pushing aside proffered hand*)
Sh—sh—shhh.

MARCELLUS

But Greg—

HAROLD

Professor Hill's the name—Harold Hill.

MARCELLUS

But Greg, what are you doing here? Whyn't you let me know you was comin'?

HAROLD

I didn't know I was myself. Besides how could I know you'd end up in a little tank town like this? You were a pretty big slicker when you were in business with me.

MARCELLUS

Too many close shaves the way you work. Besides I got me a nice comfortable girl—Ethel Toffelmier—boss's niece.

HAROLD

Gone legitimate, huh? I knew you'd come to no good.

MARCELLUS

What's the new pitch?
    (HAROLD *pantomimes conducting*)
You're not back in the band business! I heard you was in steam automobiles.

HAROLD

I was.

MARCELLUS

What happened?

HAROLD

Somebody actually invented one.

MARCELLUS

No!

HAROLD

Now give me the lowdown here, Marce.

MARCELLUS

You'll never get anywhere in the band business with these stubborn Iowans, Greg. Besides we got a stuck-up music teacher here who'll expose you before you get your grip unpacked.

HAROLD

Male or female?

MARCELLUS

The music teacher? She's the librarian—female.

HAROLD

Perfect! That's what I wanted to hear. If she passes by point her out to me.

MARCELLUS

I will. How you gonna start the pitch?

HAROLD

Same old way. Keep that music teacher off balance—and then my next step will be to get your town out of the serious trouble it's in.

MARCELLUS

River City isn't in any trouble.

HAROLD

Then I'll have to create some. I have to create a desperate need for a Boys Band. You remember—Now what's new around here. What can I use?

MARCELLUS

Nothin'—except the billiard parlor's just put in a new pool table.

31

HAROLD

They never had a pool table here before?

MARCELLUS

No—only billiards.

HAROLD

That'll do.
(*He puts down his suitcase.*)
See you later, Marce—and don't forget—music teacher.
(*He pantomimes piano playing.*)

MARCELLUS

(*Pantomiming, as he exits*)
Music teacher
(HAROLD *approaches* EWART DUNLOP *who has come out
of his grocery and is looking up at his sign.*)

HAROLD

Ah—you're Mr. Dunlop?

EWART

Yep.

HAROLD

Either you're closing your eyes to a situation you don't
wish to acknowledge or you are not aware of the calibre of
disaster indicated by the presence of a pool table in your
community.
(*As* HAROLD *continues,* PEOPLE *gather around him one
by one.*)

(Slam) Ya got	(N.B. The word
Trouble,—my friend,	*Slam* in the fol-
(Slam) Right here, I say	lowing merely de-
Trouble right here in River	notes a rhythmic
City. Why sure, I'm a	pulse)

Billiard player, certainly
Mighty proud I say I'm always
Mighty proud to say it.
(Slam) I consider that the
Hours I spend with a
Cue in my hand are
Golden. (Slam)
(Slam) Help you cultivate
Horse sense and a
Cool head and a
Keen eye. 'Jever take and try to give an iron-
    clad leave to yourself from a three-rail billiard
    shot?
(Slam) But just as I
Say it takes judgment,
Brains and maturity to
Score in a balkline
Game, *I Say* that any
Boob (Slam) kin
Take 'n' *Shove A*
Ball in a Pocket.
(Slam) And I call that
Sloth! The first big
Step on the road to the
Depths of deg-ra-
Day—I say first—
(Slam) Medicinal
Wine from a teaspoon,
Then—beer from a
Bottle. (Slam) And the
Next thing you know your
Son is playin' fer
Money in a pinch-back
Suit. (Slam) And

33

THE MUSIC MAN

List'nin to some big
Out-a-town Jasper
Hearin' him tell about
Horse-race gamblin'.
(Slam) Not a wholesome
Trottin' race. No! But a
Race where they se' down
Right on the horse!
(Slam) Like to see some
Stuck-up Jockey-boy
Settin' on DAN
PATCH? Make your bood
Boil? Well I should
Say. (Slam)
Friends, lemme tell you what I
Mean. (Slam) Ya got
One two
Three four
Five six
Pockets in a table!
Pockets that mark the
Diff'rence between a
Gentleman and a
Bum with a capital
B and that rhymes with
P and that stands fer
Pool. (Slam) And
All week long your
River City youth'll be
Frittern away, I say
Your young men'll be
Frittern (Slam)
Frittern away their
Noon-time, Suppertime,

34

Chore-time, too!
(Slam) Get the ball in the
Pocket, never mind gittin'
Dandelions pulled, or the
Screen door patched or the
Beefsteak pounded.
 (Slam) And never mind
Pumpin' any water till your
Parents are caught with the
Cistern empty on a
Saturday night and that's
Trouble, oh yes we got
Lots and lots a'
Trouble, I'm thinkin' of the
Kids in the knickerbockers
Shirt-tail young-ones
Peekin' in the Pool Hall
Winda after school,
Look Folks!
(Slam) Right here in River
City (Slam)
Trouble with a capital
T and that rhymes with
P and that stands for
Pool. (Slam) Now I know
All you folks are the
Right kind a' Parents.
(Slam) I'm going to be
Perfectly frank
(Slam) Would you like to know
What kinda conver-
Sation goes on while they're
Loafin' around that
Hall? They're tryin' out

35

Bevo, tryin' out
Cubebs, tryin' out
Tailor Mades like
Cigarette Feends!
(Slam) and braaaggin'
All about how they're gonna
Cover up a tell-tale
Breath with Sen Sen.
One fine night
(Slam) They *leave* the
Pool Hall, headin' fer the
Dance at the Arm'ry!
Libertine men and
Scarlet women! and
RAG-TIME
Shameless music that'll
Grab your son and
Your daughter with the
Arms of a jungle
Animal instinct
MASS-steria!
(Slam) Friends, the
Idle brain is the
Devil's Playground.

(*The* PEOPLE *answer* HAROLD)
Trouble (oh we've got
Trouble) Right here in River
City! (Right here in
River City!) With a capital
T and that rhymes with
P and that stands for
Pool (That stands for
Pool) We've surely got

Trouble! (We've surely got
Trouble) Right here in River
City! (Right here!)
(Slam) Gotta figger out a
Way t'keep the young ones
Moral after
School! (Our children's
Children gonna have
Trouble!)

CHORUS

Trouble—trouble
Trouble—trouble
        (*continues in background*)

HAROLD

Mothers of River City! Heed the warning before it's too
late! Watch for the tell-tale signs of corruption! The
moment your son leaves the house does he rebuckle his
knickerbockers *below the knee?* Is there a nicotine stain
on his index finger? A dime novel hidden in the corn crib?
Is he memorizing jokes out of Capt. Billy's Whiz Bang? Are
certain words creeping into his conversation? Words like
"swell" and "so's your old man"? If so, *My friends—*
    (*Slam*) (*Slam*)
                Ya got
                Trouble (Oh we've got
                Trouble) Right here in River
                City! (Right here in River
                City) With a capital
                T and that rhymes with
                P and that stands for
                Pool. (That stands for
                Pool!) We've surely got
                Trouble! (We've surely got

37

Trouble!) Right here in River
City! (Right here!)
(Slam) Remember the
Maine, Plymouth
Rock and the Golden
Rule! (Our children's
Children gonna have
Trouble!) Oh we've got
Trouble. We're in
Terrible terrible
Trouble—that game with the
Fifteen numbered
Balls is the Devil's
Tool! (Devil's
Tool!) Oh yes we got
Trouble Trouble
Trouble! (Oh yes we got
Trouble here we got big big
Trouble) With a
T! (With a capital
T) Gotta rhyme it with
P! (That rhymes with
P) And that stands for
Pool! (That stands for
Pool!)

(PEOPLE *hold for finish. As they start a reprise*
MARCELLUS *runs on excitedly, waves to*
HAROLD *and starts pantomiming wild piano
arpeggios indicating the approach of the
piano-teacher librarian*)

PEOPLE

Trouble! Oh we've got
Trouble. Right here in River

City! Right here in
River City. With a capital
T and that rhymes with
P and that stands for
Pool. That stands for
Pool! We've surely got
Trouble! We've surely got
Trouble! Right here in River
City! Right here in River
City! Gotta figger out a
Way t'keep the young ones
Moral after Schooooool.

> (*The voices collapse, the* PEOPLE *freeze in a
> "dim," the Walking Theme segues immedi-
> ately as the librarian—an attractive* YOUNG
> LADY *picked up in follow spot—hurries
> through in tempo.* HAROLD *follows her off.
> The traveller closes behind him.*)

Scene 3

TIME: *Immediately following.*

SCENE: *Before traveller depicting the street.* HAROLD
         intercepts MARIAN *re-entering. As they walk
         along the traveller, the music continues.*

                          HAROLD
    (*Offering his own handkerchief*)
Did you drop your—

                          MARIAN
No!

                          HAROLD
Didn't I meet you in—

                          MARIAN
No!

                          HAROLD
I will only be in town a short while—

                          MARIAN
Good!
    (*The porch now appears Left.* MARIAN *enters house,
    slamming door in* HAROLD'S *face.* LIGHTS FADE *fore-
    stage and come up behind scrim where we see the*
40

interior of a small house. The scrim rises. A small-fry freckle-faced eight-year-old girl is playing the piano. MRS. PAROO, *a cheerful-looking forty, continues her household chores, as* AMARYLLIS *plays, in halting tempo where she isn't sure and too fast where she is.*)

MRS. PAROO
(Calling. Speaks in Irish brogue)
That you, Daughter?

MARIAN
(Off-stage)
Yes, mama. Keep on, Amaryllis. I'll be there in a minute.
(On the down-beat of the fourth bar, AMARYLLIS *plays the melody note a half tone too high, and turns around to appeal wordlessly to* MRS. PAROO *who, in the manner of one well-accustomed to this occurrence, plays the correct note as automatically as she does her other tasks.* AMARYLLIS *happily starts over, apparently the usual step in this well-worn routine. Again the wrong note—again the correction. As* AMARYLLIS *settles herself for the third go-round,* MARIAN *enters in a hurry)*

MARIAN
Hello, Mama.
*(*MARIAN *crosses in front of piano in time to correct Amaryllis' clinker)*
Fine, dear. Now your exercises.
*(*MARIAN *kisses her mother)*

AMARYLLIS
(Replacing her piece in music roll)
Yes mom.

MRS. PAROO

I don't remember the liberry bein' open last Fourth a' July.

MARIAN

It was, Mama—all evening. Mama,* a man with a suitcase has been following me all over town.

MRS. PAROO

Oh—Who?

MARIAN

I never saw him before.

MRS. PAROO

Did he say anything?

MARIAN

He tried.

MRS. PAROO

Did you say anything?

MARIAN

Mama, of course not. Now don't dawdle, Amaryllis.
    (AMARYLLIS *begins her exercises.* MARIAN *sings along*)
        Sol do
        La re
        Ti mi, a
        Little slower and
        Please keep the fingers
        Curved as nice and
        High as you possibly can.
Don't get faster, dear.

    (MARIAN *winds metronome*)

MRS. PAROO

If you don't mind my saying so, it wouldn't have hurt you
to find out what the gentleman wanted.

MARIAN

I know what the gentleman wanted.

MRS. PAROO

What, dear?

MARIAN

You'll find it in Balzac.

MRS. PAROO

Excuse me fer livin' but I've never read it.
(AMARYLLIS *repeats in new key,* MARIAN *beats out
strict time, as she sings:*)

MARIAN

Neither has anyone
Else in this town

MRS. PAROO

There you go again with that
Same old Comment—a-
Bout the low mentality of
River City people and
Takin' it all too much to heart.

MARIAN

Now, Mama as long as the—
(*Exercise continues*)
Madison Public Library was en-
Trusted to me for the

43

Purpose of improving River
City's cultural level I
Can't help my concern that the
Ladies of River City keep ig-
Noring all my counsel and ad-
Vice.

MRS. PAROO

But darling, when a
(*Exercise continues*)
Woman's got a husband and
You've got none
Why should she take ad-
Vice from you
Even if you can quote
Balzac and Shakespeare and
All them other hifalutin'
Greeks.

MARIAN

Mama, if you
(*Exercise continues*)
Don't mind *my* sayin' so, you
Have a bad habit of
Changing ev'ry subject—

MRS. PAROO

Now I
Haven't changed the subject. I **was**
Speakin' of that stranger—

MARIAN

What
Stranger?

44

MRS. PAROO
With the suitcase who
May be your very last chance!

MARIAN
Mama! Do you
(*Exercise continues*)
     Think that I'd allow a common
     Masher—now really, Mama!
     I have my standards where
     Men are concerned, and I
     Have no intention—

MRS. PAROO
                    —I know
     All about your standards and if you
     Don't mind my sayin' so, there's
     Not a man alive who could
     Hope to measure up to that
     Blend a'Paul Bunyan, Saint
     Pat and Noah Webster you've con-
     Cocted for yourself outa your
     Irish imagination, your Iowa
     Stubbornness and your liberry fulla' books.

(*Finé chord from* AMARYLLIS)

MARIAN
(*Hands on hips, gets slightly Irish in her exasperation*)
Well, if that isn't the best I've ever heard!

AMARYLLIS
Thank you. Can I have a drink, please?

MARIAN

May I have a—

AMARYLLIS

May I have a drink, please?

MARIAN

Yes, dear.
>(*As* AMARYLLIS *starts to the sink, a ten-year-old boy with a set, sullen face enters without a word, heading for bedroom door upstage*)

MRS. PAROO

Winthrop. It's after dark.

>(WINTHROP *halts in his tracks*)
Is that a way to walk into the house?

WINTHROP

Hello
>(HE *tries to exit*)

MRS. PAROO

That won't do at all. I'll have a kiss from my boy.
>(WINTHROP *walks to his mother, stands stubbornly in her embrace for a moment, then starts out again*)
The lady over there is your sister, young man.
>(HE *repeats the uncooperative performance with* MARIAN)

AMARYLLIS

Hello, Winthrop.

>(WINTHROP *stares at the floor*)
46

MRS. PAROO

Winthrop, where's your manners.

AMARYLLIS

I'm having a party on Saturday. Will you please come?
(*Silence*)
I would especially like it very much if you'd come...
Winthrop?
(*Silence*)

MRS. PAROO

Well, Winthrop, Amaryllis asked you to her party. Are
you goin' or aren't you?

WINTHROP

No.

MRS. PAROO

No what?

WINTHROP

No, thank you.

MRS. PAROO

You know the little girl's name.

AMARYLLIS

He won't say Amaryllis because of the "s" because of his
lisp. He's ashamed.

MRS. PAROO

We know all about his lisp, Amaryllis. Well, Winthrop.

47

AMARYLLIS

I'll bet he won't say it.
> (*Tiptoeing closer to* WINTHROP, SHE *tries to peer into his face*)

WINTHROP

No thank you, Amaryllith.
> (AMARYLLIS *hops up and down giggling gleefully*)

AMARYLLIS

Amaryllith—Amaryllith.
> (SHE *moves closer to* WINTHROP, *stoops and looks up into his face as he continues to stare at his feet.* SHE *turns to* MRS. PAROO *with surprise*)

He's crying.
> (WINTHROP *bolts out of the room,* MRS. PAROO *following him.*)

Why does he get so mad at people—just because he lisps?

MARIAN

It's not only because he lisps. That's just part of it, Amaryllis.

AMARYLLIS

What's the other part?

MARIAN

Never mind, dear. It's just that he never talks very much.

AMARYLLIS

Not even to you and your mother?

MARIAN

No, dear. We all have to be a little patient.

AMARYLLIS

I'm patient. Even though he doesn't ever talk to me—but
I do him—every night—I say goodnight to him on the
evening star. You have to do it the very second you see it,
too, or it doesn't count. "Goodnight, my Winthrop, goodnight. Sleep tight."
    (SHE *starts to cry*)

MARIAN

There, darling, don't cry, you have lots of time. If not
Winthrop, there'll be someone else.

AMARYLLIS

Never! I'll end up an old maid like you.
    (SHE *catches herself*)
I'm sorry, Miss Marian. Can I play my cross-hand piece?

MARIAN

May I play my—

AMARYLLIS

May I play my cross-hand piece?

MARIAN

You may.

AMARYLLIS

See, without a sweetheart you have no one to say goodnight
to on the evening star.

MARIAN

I know, Amaryllis. For the time being just say "goodnight
my—someone." You can put the name in when the right
someone comes along.

49

AMARYLLIS

All right. It's better than nothing.

MARIAN

Yes it is... Now you can play your cross-hand piece.

AMARYLLIS

(*Settling herself*)

Now I *may* play my cross-hand piece.

(MARIAN *sings as she goes to window and looks at the evening star.*)

MARIAN

(*Sing*)

Goodnight, my someone, goodnight, my love,
Sleep tight, my someone, sleep tight, my love,
Our star is shining its brightest light
For goodnight, my love, for goodnight.
Sweet dreams be yours dear, if dreams there be
Sweet dreams to carry you close to me
I wish they may and I wish they might
Now goodnight, my someone, goodnight
True love can be whispered from heart to heart
When lovers are parted they say
But I must depend on a wish and a star
As long as my heart doesn't know who you are
Sweet dreams be yours dear, if dreams there be
Sweet dreams to carry you close to me
I wish they may and I wish they might
Now goodnight, my someone, goodnight.
Goodnight, Goodnight.

(AMARYLLIS *has come to the window as* MARIAN *is concluding the song, and sings the final lines with her.*)

DIMOUT

Scene 4

TIME: *Thirty minutes later*

AT RISE: *Interior of the Madison Gymnasium in River City High School which appears to be well-filled. It is sparingly decorated with red, white and blue bunting.* EULALIE MACKECKNIE SHINN, *fifty and gushy, costumed as* COLUMBIA *with a torch in her hand, leads the singing of "Columbia the Gem of the Ocean" as* ETHEL TOFFELMIER, *a curvaceous 35, sways at the player piano, pumping an "expressive" accompaniment. At the conclusion of the number* EULALIE *steps down from the rostrum and exits to polite applause.* MAYOR GEORGE SHINN *steps forward. He is self-important.*

SHINN

I'm sure we're all grateful to my wife, Eulalie Mackecknie Shinn for leading the singing and to Jacey Squires for his fine stereoptican slides—

(JACEY *wheels the stereoptican machine off*)

and to Ethel Toffelmier, our fine player-piano player—piano. As Mayor of River City I welcome you River Citizians to the Fourth of July exercises set up for the indoors here in Madison Gymnasium account the weather. Four score—

("*Flap-flap-flap-flap*" *interrupts the* MAYOR'S *speech. It is the end of the piano roll which* MISS TOFFELMIER *has been re-winding.* SHINN *looks around indignantly, then resumes his speech.*)

Four score—

(EWART DUNLOP *rises from his seat in front of* MAYOR *and hands him a note*)

(SHINN *reading*)

Ah—the members of the School Board will now present a patriotic tablow.

(*The three members of the School Board who are seated on the rostrum indicate he is wrong. He looks at note again*)

Oh—the members of the School Board will *not* present a patriotic tablow. Some disagreement about costumes, I suppose. Instead the Wa Tan Ye girls of the local wigwam of Heeawatha will present a spectacle my wife—

(*Catching himself he looks at notes again*)

in which my wife—

(MARIAN *hurries in with music sheets, seats herself at the piano, starts to play Indian rhythm. The* MAYOR *indicates he has not finished. She stops*)

Eulalie Mackecknie Shinn, will take a leading part.

(*He nods to* MARIAN *and she plays as six lovely corn-fed seventeenish girls appear and mount the rostrum. Each wears a feather in a head-band and they are doing an Indian war dance step.* EULALIE *precedes them in full Indian head-dress, carrying a tom-tom which she beats to* MARIAN's *Indian rhythm.* AMARYLLIS, *dressed as a Guide, follows her, struggling with a Springfield rifle.* EULALIE, *beating the Tom Tom, adjusts the Guide's sagging rifle.*)

EULALIE

(*Peering right*)

Wa Tan Ye!

GIRLS

(*Peering right*)
WA TAN YE!

EULALIE

(*again adjusting the rifle, then peering left*)
Wa Tan Ye!

GIRLS

WA TAN YE!

EULALIE

I will now count to twenty in the Indian tongue! Een teen
tuther feather fip!
(TOMMY DJILAS, *a sixteen-year-old with obviously
"poor" clothes, seated on the floor in front of* EULALIE
now sets off a large firecracker. EULALIE *swoons.*)
I'm shot, George! George! Who shot me?
(*The* MAYOR *comforts her, aiding her exit. There is
considerable disturbance.*)

CONSTABLE LOCKE

(*Rising*)
Who set off that cracker?

GRACIE SHINN

I know who did it! Tommy Djilas did it—Tommy Djilas
did it!

ALMA

Yes, it was Tommy Djilas!

CONSTABLE LOCKE

(*As* TOMMY *tries to escape*)

Tommy Djilas, I wouldn't leave if I'se you.
> (TOMMY *sits.* CONSTABLE LOCKE *joins him ominously.*)

SHINN
(Returning to rostrum)
Mrs. Shinn will recover, no thanks to a certain young ruffian who is a disgrace to our city. Four score and seven—
> (JACEY SQUIRES *re-enters, crosses to rostrum, hands* MAYOR *a note, and takes empty seat with rest of the School Board*)

"The Paine's Fireworks Spectacle, Last Days of Pomp-ee-eye will take place, providing the rain stops by nine-thirty. It'll be out to Madison Picnic Park in the far meadow, 'cross the crick from the Pest House."

EWART DUNLOP
How can it be raining? Didn't the Gazette predict fair?

JACEY SQUIRES
Sure did, Ewart, that's why we all prepared for a storm.

OLIN BRITT
The Gazette is accu'r't most a'the time and you know it, Jacey.

OLIVER HIX
You wouldn't last very long in the bankin' business bein' accur't most a'the time.
> (*A verbal free-for-all is under way.*)

SHINN
Now just a minute—let's have order here! Order! Order!
> (*The quarrel subsides. The men sit. A train whistle is heard. All the* MEN *take out their watches.*)

OLIVER

Hmm. Number eight's late again tonight.

JACEY

I make her early.

EWART

She's late alright.

OLIN

She's right on time, 'smatter'th your watch?
(*They're off again.* SHINN *struggles for order*)

SHINN

Will you members of the School Board stop bicker'n in public?

OLIN

All in the world that I said was—

SHINN

(*Hastily*)
Never mind! Four score—

HAROLD HILL

(*Half rising from where he has been an unobserved spectator*)
We heard there's a pool table in town.

MAN

Yeah—that's what I heard.

SHINN

Now just a minute—

55

MAUD

Is it a pool table or isn't it?

SHINN

Will you allow me to get on with the exercises?

MAN #2

We don't want any more exercises till we get this pool table matter settled!

HAROLD HILL

Let's protect our children.
> (CROWD *reacts*)

Resist sin and corruption.
> (CROWD *reacts*)

Smite that devil and keep our young boys pure.
> (CROWD *reacts*)

HAROLD

> (*Appearing on the podium*)

Friends
May I
Have Your attention
Please? (Slam) At-
Tention, please (Slam) (Slam) I can
Deal with this trouble
Friends, with a wave of my
Hand, this very
Hand—please ob-
Serve me if you
Will ... I'm Pro-
Fessor Harold
Hill! And I'm
Here—to organize the

River City Boys
Band! (Roll) Oh,
Think, my friends, how could
Any pool table ever
Hope to compete with a
Gold trombone?
Raaaa—raaaa
Ra-da-da-da-da
Raaa—Ra. Re-
Member, my friends, what a
Handful of trumpet players
Did to the famous
Fabled Walls of
Jericho! (Slam) Oh
Billiard Parlor
Walls come tumbling
Down! (Slam)
(Slam) (Slam) Oh a
Band'll do it, my
Friends, oh yes! I mean a
Boys Band. Do you
Hear me? (Slam) I say
River City's gotta have a
Boys Band and I
Mean she needs it to-
Day (Slam) Well, Pro-
Fessor Harold
Hill's on hand and
River City's gonna have her
Boys Band—as
Sure as the Lord made
Little green apples and that band's gonna be in uniform!
Johnny, Willy, Teddy, Fred!
And you'll see the glitter of crashing cymbals,

THE MUSIC MAN

And you'll hear the thunder of rolling drums, the shimmer
of trumpets—Tantara!
And you'll feel something akin to the electric thrill I once
enjoyed
When Gilmore (Slam) Liberatti (Slam) Pat Conway
(Slam)
The Great Creatore (Slam) W. C. Handy (Slam) and
John Philip Sousa
All came to town on the very same historic day

     (*Sing*)
Seventy six trombones led the big parade
With a hundred and ten cornets close at hand
They were followed by rows and rows
Of the finest virtuo-
sos, the cream of ev'ry famous band.
Seventy six trombones caught the morning sun
With a hundred and ten cornets right behind
There were more than a thousand reeds
Springing up like weeds
There were horns of ev'ry shape and kind
There were copper bottom tympani in horse
    platoons
Thundering, thundering all along the way
Double bell euphoniums and big bassoons
Each bassoon having his big fat say
There were fifty mounted cannon in the battery
Thundering, thundering louder than before
Clarinets of ev'ry size
And trumpeters who'd improvise
A full octave higher than the score.

    (HAROLD *parades with the* KIDS)

CHORUS

Seventy six trombones hit the counterpoint
While a hundred and ten cornets blazed away
To the rhythm of Harch—Harch—Harch
All the kids began to march
And they're marching still—right today!
> (*There is a choreographic interpolation in
> which all the* KIDS (*Dancers*) *carried along
> by the spirit of the song, pantomime instru-
> ments. The number winds up with the entire
> ensemble parading. As they disperse,* SHINN
> *corners the* SCHOOL BOARD)

SHINN

Men, this calls for emergency action. That man is a spell
binder. I haven't seen Iowa people get so excited since the
night Frank Gotch and Strangular Lewis lay on the mat
for three and a half hours without moving a muscle! Never
mind! I want his credentials.
> (TOMMY DJILAS, *being escorted out by* CONSTABLE
> LOCKE, *suddenly cuts and runs. Reversing his field he
> runs into* HAROLD *who holds him*)

Grab that hoodlum! He almost blew up Mrs. Shinn!

CONSTABLE

Thank you, Professor. Have to make an example of him.
Ringleader, you know. What he does the gang does.

TOMMY

Jeely Kly, lemme go.

SHINN

Ya wild kid ya. Hanging around my oldest girl. His father is one a'them day laborers south a'town. Ya wild kid, ya.
(*To* HAROLD)
Taggin' down Main Street after my oldest girl last Sunday.

TOMMY

I wasn't either taggin'.

SHINN

Don't you counterdict me!

TOMMY

We 'uz just walkin' together, Jeely Kly—

SHINN

You watch your frazolagy! I know what you'uz doin', my little Gracie seen ya. Now you stay away from my oldest girl or you'll hear from me till who laid the rails! Hill, I'll talk to you Monday morning about this band thing. Over't City Hall. Ten o'clock sharp.
(*Aside as he exits*)
Men, I want that spell-binder's credentials.

HAROLD

(*As* CONSTABLE *starts off with* TOMMY)
Constable, I'll be responsible for the boy.

CONSTABLE

You don't know this kid—he's tough, and he's got his gang waitin' outside.

HAROLD

Oh, I'll be careful. Tommy, like to talk to you about the band.

TOMMY

Aw gee, Professor, that's for the little kids.

HAROLD

I'm not talking about you playing in the band. You're mechanically minded, aren't you? Ever do anything with perpetual motion?

TOMMY

(*Sullenly*)

Nearly had it a couple times.

HAROLD

You did? You're my man! Do you realize nobody has **ever** invented a music-holder for a marching piccolo player?
(*He holds arms in piccolo playing position.*)
No place to hang the music.

TOMMY

(*Impressed*)

Jeely Kly! Wonder where I could get some wire from.

HAROLD

Look in your cellar, that's where people keep wire.
(TOMMY *starts tearing out. The* CONSTABLE *makes a move,* HAROLD *restrains him.*)
Oh Tommy!

TOMMY

(*Stopping in midflight*)

Yessir?
(CONSTABLE LOCKE *reacts in astonishment at the "sir"*)

61

HAROLD

(Aside to CONSTABLE*)*

Now, Constable, I'll show you how to break up a gang.
(Looks around, sees several Wa Tan Ye girls about to exit, beckons to the last one, very pretty, pink and sixteen)
Oh young lady. Oh miss—
(She turns)
What's your name?

ZANEETA

(Approaching)

Zaneeta. I didn't have any idea you was beckoning to me. Ye Gods.

HAROLD

Do you know Tommy Djilas?

ZANEETA

Well, I—

HAROLD

Tommy, this is Zaneeta. Escort the young lady home.

ZANEETA

Only excepting I'm not going home. I have to go't the Liberry, Ye Gods.

HAROLD

Then escort the young lady home by way of the library—
(Takes out money)
by way of the candy kitchen.

TOMMY

(Grinning)

Yes sir. Do I hafta?

HAROLD

You hafta.

TOMMY

Yes sir.

ZANEETA

(*As she and* TOMMY *exit*)
Ye Gods.

CONSTABLE

Professor, you're a pretty bright young fellow. You made a couple mistakes, though.

HAROLD

Oh?

CONSTABLE

The Mayor happens to own the Billiard Parlor and that new pool table.

HAROLD

Oh. What was my other mistake?

CONSTABLE

That Zaneeta. She's the Mayor's oldest girl.
(*As* HAROLD *starts to cross to the* LADIES *who have entered Right, the* SCHOOL BOARD *approaches him from Left*)

EWART

(*The second tenor*)
Just a minute—Professor Hill. We'd like to have your credentials. We're the School Board.

63

OLIN

(*The bass*) (*Contradicting*)
Academic certificates.

OLIVER

(*The baritone, to* OLIN, *with irritation*)
Nothing of the kind!

EWART

(*The 2nd tenor, to* OLIVER, *irascibly*)
We need letters and papers!

JACEY

(*The high tenor, to the* OTHERS, *nastily*)
Make him put up a bond!

HAROLD

What am I *hearing?*
(*Whirling back to* OLIN, *blows pitch pipe*)
Say (*sings on low note*) Ice Creeeem.

OLIN

Ice Cream, but I don't sing young man, if that's what
you're—

HAROLD

All right, talk then. (*Low*) Down here!

OLIN

Ice Cream.

HAROLD

Talk slow!

OLIN

(*In a rich rolling bass*)
Ice Creeeem.

HAROLD

See? Singing is only sustained talking.
    (*Pointing to* OLIVER—*sings on a baritone note*)
Now youuuuu.

OLIVER

(*In a full baritone*)
Ice Creeeeeem.

HAROLD

(*To* EWART)
Now youuuuu. Right heeeer.

EWART

Ice Creeeeem.

HAROLD

(*Points skyward to* JACEY)
Now, you, sir!

JACEY

(*On the high note*)
Ice Creeeeeemmmmmmm.

HAROLD

(*Crossing to the ladies*)
Ladies, from now on you'll never see one of those men
without the other three.

EULALIE

Oh, Professor, you're wrong! Why they've hated each other for fifteen years.

JACEY, EWART, OLIN, OLIVER

(*Behind* HAROLD's *back they hit a gorgeous chord*)
Ice Creeeeeemmmmmm!
(HAROLD *smugly joins the* MEN *as they are shaking hands all around and congratulating each other*)

HAROLD

(*Sings, pointing at* QUARTET)
How can there be

QUARTET

any sin in sincere
Where is the good in goodbye?
Your apprehensions confuse me dear
Puzzle and mystify
Mystify
(MARIAN *exits with* HAROLD *in pursuit. The* LADIES *move upstage as the lights dim and the* QUARTET *moves down in front of closing traveller in a follow spot*)
Tell me
What can be fair in farewell, dear
While one single star shines above
How can there be any sin in sincere?
Aren't we sincerely in love?
Oh we're in love.
(*As* QUARTET *holds its last gorgeous note we* BLACKOUT. *The music segues to Walking Theme.*)

Scene 5

TIME: *Immediately following*

AT RISE: *Lights come up on the street in front of the*
Library
Walking Theme accompanies MARIAN'S *en-*
trance. HAROLD *is following.*

HAROLD

I don't suppose you live alone, or anything?

MARIAN

No!

HAROLD

I've got some wonderful caramels over't the hotel if you'd—
(MARIAN *and Music stop abruptly*)

MARIAN

Mister Hill.

HAROLD

Professor Hill.

MARIAN

Professor of what? At what college do they give a degree
for annoying women on the street like a Saturday night
rowdy at a public dance hall?

HAROLD

Oh I wouldn't know about that. I'm a Conservatory man myself. Gary Indiana Gold Medal Class of '05.

MARIAN

Even should that happen to be true does that give you the right to follow me around wherever I go? Another thing, Mister Hill, I'm not as easily mesmerized or hoodwinked as some people in this town and I think it only fair to warn you that I have a shelf full of reference books in there which may very well give me some interesting information about you.

(*She exits into the Library. As* HAROLD *starts after her,* MARCELLUS *enters*)

MARCELLUS

Hey, Gregory!

HAROLD

Oh hi, Marcellus. And don't call me Greg.

MARCELLUS

How'd you make out with the music teacher?

HAROLD

Scrumptious. Ate out of my hand the minute I tipped my hat.

MARCELLUS

She did! Boy, did you cut a swath over't the high school tonight. For a minute even I thought you knew somethin' about leadin' a band. Just like when you used to imitate that band-concert fellow back in Joplin.

HAROLD

Yeah!

(*He pantomimes conducting*)

Aw—kid stuff. I'm in rare form these days, son. Just you keep your eyes on me for the next four weeks.

MARCELLUS

Four weeks! It only used to take *ten days* for the instruments to arrive.

HAROLD

It still does. But it takes four weeks for the uniforms.

MARCELLUS

Oh, no, Greg! You haven't added uniforms!!

HAROLD

Uniforms *and* instruction books.

MARCELLUS

Instruction books! But you can't pass yourself off as a music professor—I mean, not for any four weeks.

HAROLD

(*Reproachfully*)

Marce—

MARCELLUS

But you don't know one note from another.

HAROLD

I have a revolutionary new method called the Think System where you don't bother with notes.

MARCELLUS

But in four weeks the people will want to hear the music!
You'll have to lead a band.

HAROLD

But when the uniforms arrive they forget everything else—
at least long enough for me to collect and leave. Oh this is
a refined operation, son, and I've got it timed right down to
the last wave of the brakeman's hand on the last train out'a
town. And now, Mr. Washburn, if you'll excuse me—

MARCELLUS

Gonna line yourself up a little canoodlin' huh?

HAROLD

Well—

MARCELLUS

Say, I could fix you up with Ethel's sister—lovely girl—
teaches Sunday School—

HAROLD

No wide-eyed, eager, wholesome innocent Sunday School
teachers for me. That kinda girl spins webs no spider ever—
listen, boy—

HAROLD

(*Sings*)
A girl who
Trades on all that purity merely wants to
Trade my independence for her security. The
Only affirmative she will file re-
Fers to marching down the aisle. No

70

Golden, glorious, gleaming pristine goddess—
    No sir!
For no Diana do I play faun. I can tell you that
    right now.
I snarl, I hiss: How can ignorance be compared
    to bliss?
I spark, I fizz for the lady who knows what time
    it is
I cheer, I rave for the virtue I'm too late to save
The sadder-but-wiser girl for me.
No bright-eyed blushing breathless baby-doll baby
    Not for me. That kinda
Child Ties Knots No sailor ever knew
I prefer to take a chance
On a more adult romance
No dewy young miss who keeps resisting all the
    time she keeps insisting
No wide-eyed wholesome innocent female. No sir.
Why she's the fisherman, I'm the fish, you see?—
    PLOP!
I flinch, I shy, when the lass with the delicate air
    goes by
I smile, I grin, when the gal with a touch of sin
    walks in
I hope, I pray, for Hester to win just one more "A"
The sadder-but-wiser girl's the girl for me
The sadder-but-wiser girl for me.

> (HAROLD *is starting towards the library as the*
> WOMEN *come chattering in,* EULALIE *hanging*
> *back.* MARCELLUS *escapes.* HAROLD *is sur-*
> *rounded*)

ALMA

Oh, Professor Hill, we're all agog—simply agog!

MAUD

On the que veev!

MRS. SQUIRES

Everyone's so excited about the band.

ETHEL

(*Loud voice*)
I'm Ethel Toffelmier. The pianola girl?

MAUD

And this is Mrs. Squires, and Mrs. Hix. And of course you
met Eulalie Mackecknie Shinn? Our Mayor's wife? Isn't
it exciting, Eulalie?

EULALIE

Oh, I couldn't say. I *could not say*. Oh no. I could not say,
at this time. My husband will wish to investigate, I'm sure.
And naturally I'm reticent. Oh yes, I'm reticent.

HAROLD

Of *course*, Mrs. Shinn, I understand. But you see, part of
my music plans include a committee on the dance and—no
wait—wait! Do that again, Mrs. Shinn!
    (*She looks behind her, mystified*)
Your foot! The way you raised it, just now!

MRS. SHINN

    (*Lifting foot slightly*)
Oh. Well. I have a bunion there that bothers—

HAROLD

Ohhh what grace! What natural flow of rhythm! What
expression of line and movement!

72

EULALIE

Mister Hill!

HAROLD

You *must* accept the chairmanship of the Ladies Auxiliary for the Classic dance, mustn't she, ladies?

THE WOMEN

Oh yes! Please! You must, Eulalie.

HAROLD

Every move you make, Mrs. Shinn, bespeaks Del Sarte. Will you—will you? Say yes, Mrs. Shinn!

MRS. SHINN

(*Moving forward amid flutters, she murmurs*)
Eulalie *Mackecknie* Shinn—ah—well! I—ah—that is— Dancing! Well!

HAROLD

Then you accept?

EULALIE

Yes indeed! And I would like to say—

HAROLD

Thank you. Now the young lady who plays the piano— Marian Paroo, I believe?
(*The* LADIES *all gasp and instantly huddle.*)
After all she is the librarian.

ALMA

Pickalittletalkalittlepickalittletalkalittle
Cheepcheepcheep talkalot pickalittlemore

ALMA AND ETHEL

Pickalittletalkalittlepickalittletalkalittle
Cheepcheepcheep talkalot pickalittlemore

ALL

Pickalittletalkalittlepickalittletalkalittle
Cheepcheepcheep talkalot pickalittlemore
Pickalittletalkalittlepickalittletalkalittle
Cheepcheepcheepcheepcheepcheepcheepcheep

SECOND CHORUS
(Continues as background to following dialogue)

MAUD

Professor, her kind of woman doesn't belong on any committee. Of course I shouldn't tell you this but she advocates *dirty books.*

HAROLD

Dirty books!

ALMA

Chaucer!

ETHEL

Rabelais!

EULALIE

Bal-zac!

MAUD

And the *worst* thing—of course I shouldn't tell you this but...

74

ALMA

I'll tell.

ETHEL

The man lived on my street. Let me tell.

EULALIE
(*Grabs the ball determinedly*)
Stop! I'll tell.
(*Everything stops*)
She made brazen overtures to a man who never had a friend
in this town till *she* came here—old Miser Madison.

HAROLD
(*Puzzled*)
Miser Madison. Madison Gymnasium, Madison Picnic Park,
Madison Hospital—that Miser Madison?

MAUD

Exactly. Who'd he think he was anyway?

HAROLD

Well I should say. Show off. Gave the town the library too,
didn't he?

ETHEL

That's just it. When he died he left the liberry building to
the city—

MAUD

But he left all the books to her!

75

EULALIE

She was seen going and coming from his place.

ALMA

Oh yes. Oh yes.
    (LADIES *continue with* "*Pickalittle*")
        That woman made
        Brazen overtures
        (Slam) (Slam) With a
        Gild-edge guaran-
        Tee. She had a
        Golden glint in her
        Eye and a silver
        Voice with a counterfeit
        Ring. (Slam) Just
        Melt her down and you'll reveal a
        Lump of lead as cold as steel
        Here! (Thump) where a
        Woman's heart should
        Be!

EULALIE, ALMA, MAUD, ETHEL, MRS. SQUIRES

    He
    Left River City the
    Library building but he
    Left all the books to
    Her!

ALMA

Chaucer!

ETHEL

Rabelais!

EULALIE

Bal-zac!
(THE LADIES *all continue "Pickalittle" forte as* HAROLD *tries to escape.* THE QUARTET *enters.*)

JACEY

Just a minute here! We need your credentials.

HAROLD

Yes, of course, I have just what you want over at the Hotel. Come with me.
(*As they start to follow him, he turns back to the* LADIES *who are still singing "Pickalittle."*)
Goodnight ladies.
(*They "Cheep cheep cheep" at him. He turns to* QUARTET *and sings contrapuntally*)
Goodnight ladies,
(THE QUARTET *immediately picks it up and* HAROLD *escapes into the Library as the* LADIES *and* QUARTET *finish the number together, the* LADIES *still singing "Pickalittle."*)

QUARTET

Goodnight ladies, Goodnight ladies
We're going to leave you now
Farewell ladies, Farewell ladies, Farewell ladies,
We're going to leave you now.

BLACKOUT

Scene 6

TIME: *Immediately following.*

The scrim becomes transparent. We see the interior of the library. The scrim flies. MARIAN *is seen at desk stamping books.* HAROLD *sneaks in and places his hat under her stamper. She is startled.*

HAROLD

It's all right—I know everything and it doesn't make any difference.

MARIAN

What are you talking about?

HAROLD

You were probably very young—any one can make a mistake—

MARIAN

What—

HAROLD

No apologies—no explanations, please. I'll only be in town a short time and
(*Chuckles*)
the sadder, but wiser girl for me.

78

MARIAN

Will you please make your selection and leave.

HAROLD

I have.

MARIAN

(*Looking for book*)
Well? What do you want to take out?

HAROLD

(*Loudly*)
The librarian.

MARIAN

Quiet *please!*

HAROLD

(MARIAN *turns her back;* HAROLD *whispers*)
The librarian. You're not listening, Marian.
(*He takes a drawstring bag out of pocket*)
Look!
(*He sings*)
Ma-a-a-a-rian.
(*Speaks*)
Marbles. Six steelies, eight aggies, a dozen peewees and one
big glassie with an American flag in the middle. I think I'll
drop 'em.

MARIAN

No!

79

Shh!

    (*Threatens her with bag. Sings*)

        Madam Librarian

        What can I do, my dear, to catch your ear

        I love you madly, madly, Madam Librarian...
            Marian

        Heaven help us if the library caught on fire

        And the Volunteer Hose Brigademen

        Had to whisper the news to Marian...Madam
            Librarian!

        What can I say, my dear, to make it clear

        I need you badly, badly, Madam Librarian...
            Marian

        If I stumbled and I busted my what-you-may-
            call-it

        I could lie on your floor unnoticed

        Till my body had turned to carrion...Madam
            Librarian.

        Now in the moonlight

        A man could sing it

        In the moonlight

        And a fellow would know that his darling

        Had heard ev'ry word of his song

        With the moonlight

        Helping along

        But when I try in here to tell you dear

        I love you madly, madly, Madam Librarian...
            Marian

        It's a long lost cause I can never win

        For the civilized world accepts as unforgivable sin

        Any talking out loud with any librarian

        Such as Marian...Madam Librarian.

(*The* BALLET *commences in which* HAROLD
and MARIAN *and the* READERS *in the library
participate.*)

HAROLD

But when I try in here to tell you dear
I love you madly, madly, Madam Librarian ...
    Marian
It's a long lost cause I can never win
For the civilized world accepts as unforgivable
    sin
Any talking out loud with any librarian
Such as Marian ... Madam Librarian.
The Ladies Dance Committee meets Tuesday nights.
    (*Opening "marble" bag, he offers it to her*)
Marshmallow?
    (*Harold catches* MARIAN *off guard and kisses her on
the cheek.* MARIAN *is shocked into reality. He stuffs a
marshmallow in his mouth and* MARIAN *has now had it,
giving him a round-house slap which* HAROLD *ducks. It
catches* TOMMY DJILAS *full on the ear. We black out
and bring in the Library Exterior*)

Scene 7

TIME: *The following Saturday noon*

AT RISE: TOMMY & HAROLD *are seen in front of the traveller, Stage Left.*

HAROLD

Well, Tommy, we've had a pretty good morning. Eleven sales out of twelve tries. Tell you what— It's almost noon, you better go home and get some dinner. I'll try a couple by myself.

TOMMY

G'bye, Professor.

HAROLD

Thanks Tommy.
> *("76 Trombones" is heard for bridge music as* HAROLD *approaches a door, Stage Right. It is an impressive doorway.* HAROLD *rings doorbell.* SHINN *comes hurrying down the street, goes to door, starts to unlock it— realizes* HAROLD's *presence.)*

SHINN

Just a minute here. Are you soliciting? You haven't got a license.

HAROLD

Why no, Mayor Shinn, I collect doorbells. This particular specimen has an unusual tone quality that—

82

SHINN

Flattery will not avail you. Soliciting is statutory in this county—malfeasance without a permit. Why haven't you been down't City Hall with your references?

HAROLD
(*Stepping down to* SHINN)
Just missed you I—. Mr. Mayor! Your hand—oh no!

SHINN

What, what—

HAROLD
(*Spreads* SHINN's *fingers*)
That spread of the little finger! It's hereditary!

SHINN

Oh it is—what does that mean?

HAROLD

It means that your son's little finger is perfectly situated to operate the spit-valve on a B flat flugel horn!

SHINN
(*Wide eyed*)
Is that good?

HAROLD

Good! It means that America has at last produced an artist who can flugle the Minute Waltz in 50 seconds.

SHINN

How could I get one of those horns?

83

HAROLD

(*Quick with order blank*)

Sign here, Mr. Mayor. That'll be seventeen dollars import fee.

SHINN

(*Signing*)

Yes sir. Just think I could'a missed this whole—

(*Stops suddenly*)

I haven't got any son! You unscrypulous flew-by-night, you unflypulous—you be down't City Hall with your By God papers at three o'clock.

HAROLD

You mean this afternoon?

SHINN

I couldn't make myself any plainer if I'se a Quaker on his day off!

("*76 Trombones*" *tag hits and fades*)

BLACKOUT

Scene 8

TIME: *That evening*

AT RISE: The Paroos' porch. MRS. PAROO *is sitting on the
porch rocking.* WINTHROP *is hiding behind her
chair.* HAROLD *has entered at rise.*

HAROLD

Mrs. Paroo, do you realize you have the facial character-
istics of a cornet virtuoso?

MRS. PAROO

I don't know if I understand you entirely, Professor.

HAROLD

If your boy has that same firm chin, and those splendid
cheek muscles—By George! Not that he could ever be
really great, you understand, but—

MRS. PAROO

Oh, is that so. And in the name of St. Bridget, why not?

HAROLD

Well—you see all the really great cornet players were
Irish—O'Clark, O'Mendez, O'Klein—

MRS. PAROO

But Professor, we are Irish!

HAROLD

No! No! Really? That clinches it! Sign here, Mrs. Paroo.
Your boy was born to play the cornet!

(*She signs in a daze.* WINTHROP *has followed her and
is still hiding behind her*)

Fine, fine. That will be seven dollars earnest money.
Nothing more due until the first installment payable at
opening of band practice.

(MRS. PAROO *locates money from about her person.*)

Ah thank you. And of course, I'll need the boy's measurements for his band uniform.

MRS. PAROO

His uniform!

(WINTHROP *falls off the porch in excitement.*)

HAROLD

Hello, son.

(WINTHROP *picks himself up and starts to run.* HAROLD
stops him.)

Certainly his uniform. And there won't be a penny due till
delivery, which gives him four weeks to enjoy, to antici-
pate, to imagine, at no cost whatever. Never allow the
demands of tomorrow to interfere with the pleasures and
excitement of today.

WINTHROP

(*Drawing an imaginary line down the outside of his
leg*)

Would it have. . . . a. . . . a. . . . ?

HAROLD

A stripe? Certainly, my boy, a wide red stripe on each side.
What do you think of that?

(WINTHROP *drops his eyes suddenly and runs off*)

MRS. PAROO

You'll have to excuse Winthrop, Professor. We can't get
him to say three words a day even to us. And if you get
him to play in the band you'll have St. Michael's own way
with you. But if anybody can do it I'll bet you can. Out of
a crowd I'll pick you for a hod-carrying, clay-pipe smokin'
shamrock-wearin, harp-playin' Mavorneen-pinchin' Tara's
hall minstrel-singin' Irishman! Be-gob and be-jabbers!
Where are ye from, me bye?

HAROLD

Gary, Indiana.

MRS. PAROO

I knew it! Gar—. Where did you say?

HAROLD

Gary Indiana. In fact Gary Conservatory was my Alma
Mater.

MRS. PAROO

Was she now?

HAROLD
(*Aware of Marian's approach*)

Why yes—Gold Medal Class of '05. Hodado, Miss Paroo.

MARIAN

Hodado, Mr. Hill.

HAROLD

Of course! Paroo. I thought the name sounded familiar.
(*Sotto*)
I've tried to see you since the other night, but—

MRS. PAROO

He wants to put Winthrop in the band!

MARIAN

We're not interested, mama.

MRS. PAROO

But Marian, the boy might have his father's musical gift. He does have my jaw, you know.

HAROLD

Oh—your husband musical? Well, I'd like to have a talk with him. I'm sure we—

MARIAN

Do you burst in on everyone's home like this? Prying into personal affairs? We're not interested.

MRS. PAROO

Marian!

HAROLD

    (Cheerfully)

Well, that's one for and one against. Now why not let the boy's father decide?

MARIAN

The boy's father is dead. Anything else?

HAROLD

Oh, I'm sorry. But that's all the more reason why your brother should have something like this—

88

MARIAN

My brother is a ten-year-old problem child who can't understand why his father was taken away. Would you care to explain it to him? He's been brooding about it for two years. As to your musical tricks, why don't you go into business with some nice carnival man who sells gold-painted watches and glass diamond rings?

HAROLD

Musical tricks? Well Miss Paroo, I hardly—
> (*Without response* MARIAN *exits into house.* MRS.
> PAROO *stands speechless.*)

I get the feeling she likes the idea. Oh a little cautious perhaps but I admire that in a woman. Just keep me alive and I'll be back later in the week.

MRS. PAROO

One moment, Professor Hill. About the boy's measurements. I make all his clothes. Sleeve 21, Waist 18, Croutch, 14—

HAROLD

Fine, that's all I need. Now I must get back to the Hotel.

MRS. PAROO

Professor, I do hope you'll excuse Marian. She's not really—

HAROLD

Please. Don't worry about a thing. I'm sure that at heart she's as lovely as yourself. Good day to you, Widda Paroo.

MARIAN

> (*Returning to porch with embroidery and slip of
> paper*)

Has he gone?

89

MRS. PAROO

He has. And I hope not forever. Darlin' don't you ever think of your future? Gary Indiana Conservation Class of '05—Now darlin'—

MARIAN

Now mama. Surely a girl's future doesn't depend on encouraging every fast-talking, self-centered, woman-chasing travelling man who comes to town. And the fact that he claims his commodity is music does not, in this particular case, impress me.

MRS. PAROO

All right, darlin', all right. Only it's a well-known principle that if you keep the flint in one drawer and the steel in another, you'll never strike much of a fire.

MARIAN

Mama!
    (*Calling*)
Winthrop! Winthrop, I know you're there.
    (WINTHROP *comes slowly to porch*)
Please go to the library and ask Miss Grubb to give you the book I set aside. It's the Indiana State Educational Journal 1890-1910. It's a large brown volume with black corners.

WINTHROP

Do I hafta?

MARIAN

You won't have to talk to anyone. I've written it all down.
    (*She gives him paper. He goes*)
Thank you dear.

MRS. PAROO

Now what are you up to? Why do you need books at this hour of the night?

MARIAN

I have a feeling the Indiana Journal may help me poke some large holes in the Professor's claims.

MRS. PAROO

Well, I give up. At your age if you don't mind my sayin' so, what kinda white knight do you expect to come ridin' along?

MARIAN

Well, I'm not waiting for Luther Greiner who backs me into the Ancient History shelf every time he comes into the Library.

MRS. PAROO

He does?

MARIAN

Or Ed Gammidge and that buggy of his with the removable back seat. But I'm not waiting for a man in shining white armor either.
    (*Sings*)
        My White Knight
        Not a Lancelot, nor an angel with wings
        Just someone to love me
        Who is not ashamed of a few nice things
        My White Knight
        What my heart would say if it only knew how
        Please dear Venus
        Show me now.

THE MUSIC MAN

All I want is a plain man,
All I want is a modest man,
A quiet man, a gentle man
A straightforward and honest man
To sit with me in a cottage somewhere in the state
    of Iowa.
And I would like him to be more int'rested in me
Than he is in himself,
And more int'rested in us than in me.
And if occasion'ly he'd ponder
What makes Shakespeare and Beethoven great
Him I could love till I die.
Him I could love till I die.
My White Knight
Not a Lancelot, nor an angel with wings
Just someone to love me
Who is not ashamed of a few nice things
My White Knight
Let me walk with him where the others ride by
Walk—and love him
Till I die.
Till I die.

              DIMOUT

Scene 9

TIME: *Noon, the following Saturday.*

AT RISE: Center of Town, exterior. ZANEETA *is crossing
             followed by* TOMMY *wearing "his invention."*

TOMMY

(*Calling*)
... Zaneeta ... Hey Zaneeta—
    (SHE *stops and turns*)

ZANEETA

Tommy, papa and mama are sitting right there in the bank.
Ye Gods!

TOMMY

All right, then meet me after supper.

ZANEETA

I can't. It's Epworth League night. Meet you where?

TOMMY

The footbridge.

ZANEETA

You see? Isn't that just what I said? Last time the lumber
yard and now the footbridge. And where will you meet
me after that? In the Black Hole of Calcutta? Ye Gods.

93

TOMMY

I only want to show you my invention.

ZANEETA

What invention?

TOMMY

My music holder for a marching piccolo player. It still has a couple of minor flaws; see, when you keep it tight enough to hold the music steady you cut off the circulation and you can't wiggle your fingers. Meanwhile—
(He demonstrates how close it would be in playing position)
You *could* go blind.

ZANEETA
(Gestures in alarm at Oliver Hix' office)
Tommy: It's Papa!
(TOMMY *leaves in a hurry as* SHINN & EULALIE *enter*)

SHINN

Is that the first thing I said, or not?

EULALIE

Yes, George.

SHINN

Yes! The very *first thing I said* or I'll eat hay with the horse! Get that Spell-binder's credentials, I said, morning of Jew-ly Fourth, Nineteen and Twelve. And now look! My wife is off dancing at any and all hours instead of in the home—

EULALIE

But George—
94

SHINN

—the School Board is singin' up street and down alley instead of tending to city matters, my oldest girl is boodleing around with some wild kid and my business has fallen off so far I can't find the balance sheet.

MARIAN
(*Entering with brown book*)
Mayor Shinn, I've found something very interesting in this book about Professor Hill's Alma Mater.

SHINN

His who?

MARIAN

His university.

SHINN

I know all about that. In fact, that's the only thing I can ever get out of him—Gary Conservatory, class of aught-five.

MARIAN

If you'll just take time to read a little bit about the Conservatory I don't think you'll have to look further. It's on page . .
(HORSE MUSIC)
(GRACIE SHINN *rushes on*)

GRACIE

Papa! The Wells Fargo Wagon is just comin' up from the depot!

95

ALL

(*In hushed anticipation*)
The Wells Fargo Wagon!

SHINN

A likely story! At this hour of the day? Nonsense! ... The
Wells Fargo Wagon?

GRACIE

It could be the band instruments!

SHINN

The band instruments!
(THE PEOPLE *form, looking up the street listening
for the horse's hooves which are now heard plainly in
the music.*)

THE PEOPLE

(*Sing*)
    O-ho the Wells Fargo Wagon is a-comin' down
        the street
    Oh please let it be for me
    O-ho the Wells Fargo Wagon is a-comin' down
        the street
    I wish, I wish I knew what it could be.

1ST VOICE

I got a box of maple sugar on my birthday

2ND VOICE

In March I got a grey mackinaw

3RD VOICE

And once I got some grapefruit from Tampa

4TH VOICE

Montgom'ry Ward sent me a bathtub and a cross-cut saw

THE PEOPLE

O-ho the Wells Fargo Wagon is a-comin' now
Is it a prepaid surprise or C.O.D.

5TH VOICE

It could be curtains

6TH VOICE

Or dishes

7TH VOICE

Or a double boiler

8TH VOICE

Or it could be

THE PEOPLE

Yes, it could be
Yes, you're right it surely could be

8TH VOICE

Somethin' special

THE PEOPLE

Somethin' very very special now

8TH VOICE

Just for me

THE PEOPLE

O-ho the Wells Fargo Wagon is a-comin' down
the street,
Oh don't let him pass my door!
O-ho the Wells Fargo Wagon is a-comin' down
the street,
I wish I knew what he was comin' for.

9TH VOICE

I got some salmon from Seattle last September

10TH VOICE

And I expect a new rockin' chair

11TH VOICE

I hope I get my raisins from Fresno

QUARTET

The D.A.R. have sent a cannon for the courthouse square.
(WINTHROP *breaks through the crowd and as the people
turn to look at him in amazement, he sings*)

WINTHROP

O-ho, the Wellth Fargo Wagon ith a-comin' now
I don't know how I can ever wait to thee
It could be thumpin' for thumone who ith
No relathion but
It could be thump'n thpethyul
Jutht for me!

PEOPLE

O-ho, you Wells Fargo Wagon keep a-comin'
O-ho, you Wells Fargo Wagon keep a-comin'

O-ho you Wells Fargo Wagon Don't you dare
to make a stop
Until you stop for me.
> (MARIAN *pushes her way through the crowd
> to crush* WINTHROP *in an embrace as the*
> CROWD *cheers Wagon's arrival.*)

PEOPLE

Ray-yy!

DRIVER

Whoa!

WINTHROP

It'th the band inthtrumenth!
> (HAROLD *riding in wagon jumps down, carrying gold
> cornet which he brings to* WINTHROP)

HAROLD

Here you are, Winthrop.

WINTHROP

My cornet! Gee thankth, Profethor!

HAROLD

> (*Returning to wagon*)

Men! You will each receive individual instruction in due
course. In the meantime stay off the streets—get acquainted
with your instruments and think about the Minuet in G.
La de da de da de da de da—

BOYS

> (*Exiting*)

La de da, La de da.

WINTHROP

Thithter! Thithter! Ithn't thith the motht thcrumpthyuth tholid gold thing you ever thaw. I never thought I'd ever thee anything tho thcrumpthyuth ath thith thcrumpthyuth tholid gold thing! Oh thithter!

SHINN

Round one for you Mister Hill, but I better hear some by God tootin' out'a them horns in pretty short order or I'll see you in front a'the grand jury over't the County Seat.

(*Approaching* MARIAN)

Now Miss Marian, about that book—

(MARIAN *tears page out of book as* EULALIE *calls* SHINN)

EULALIE

Come, George! Tempus fugits.

SHINN

(*Turning to her*)

You watch your frazolagy. I've got to get something from the librarian.

(*Crosses to* MARIAN)

About that book—

(MARIAN *hands him the book, hiding torn out page.* SHINN & EULALIE *exit.* HAROLD *catches* MARIAN'S *look which is changing from gratitude to adoration.*)

HAROLD

(*Coming over to her*)

The Ladies Dance Committee meets Tuesday nights at the High School.

(THEY *hold the look as the Orchestra, with "My White Knight," swells to climax.*)

CURTAIN

END OF FIRST ACT

ACT TWO

Scene 1

TIME: *Evening. The following Tuesday.*

*AT RISE: Madison Gymnasium. The Ladies Auxiliary
Committee is practicing for the Ice Cream
Sociable.* MAUD, ALMA, ETHEL, MRS. SQUIRES *and*
EULALIE *are dressed in "girls" basket-ball
bloomers, black stockings and tennis shoes, Peter
Thomson blouses and black hair ribbons. At
rise,* MARIAN *is pumping "Rustle of Spring" at
the player piano as the* LADIES *circle with books
balanced on their heads.* THE QUARTET *is on one
side of the stage dressed in Indian regalia.*

EULALIE
Lovely, ladies, lovely. Now turn. Take the body with you.
Lovely. Now let's have a try at our Grecian Urns. One
Grecian Urn . . . . . . Two Grecian Urns . . . . and a
fountain. . . . . trickle, trickle, trickle. Splendid, ladies. I pre-
dict that our Del Sarte display will be the highlight of the
Ice Cream Sociable. Now gentlemen, if you're ready—
(THE QUARTET *comes over and takes positions*)
And ladies, remember—don't make me tell you again. Al-
ways keep your face to the audience. All right, Mr. Dunlop.
(EWART *blows pitchpipe.* MAUD *pops out from behind
him,* EULALIE *motions her back.* THE QUARTET *sings
as the* LADIES *pantomime appropriately.*)

EWART

It's you in the sunrise, it's you in my cup

JACEY

It's you all the way into town

OLIVER

It's your sweet "Hello dear" that sets me up

QUARTET

And it's your "Got to go dear" that gets me down
It's you on my pillow
In all of my dreams
Till once more the morning breaks through
What words could be saner or truer or plainer
Than it's you, it's you

EULALIE

Smile, girls, smile.

JACEY

Yes it's you

QUARTET

Oh yes it's you

MARCELLUS

(*Trying to hold* KIDS *back at the door*)
Please kids, Mrs. Shinn will have my head.

EULALIE

Mr. Washburn, we are entitled to five more minutes.

MARCELLUS

If you think you can hold these kids back, go ahead.
(THE KIDS *burst in excitedly as* EULALIE *fights her way
through them and exits right.* THE QUARTET *and the*
LADIES *quickly get out of the way*)

TOMMY

Start her up, Mr. Washburn! Wait till you see the new
steps Professor Hill taught us.

MARCELLUS

All right! What'll it be?

TOMMY

The Shipoopi!

KIDS

Shipoopi!
(*They form Virginia Reel lines*)

MARCELLUS

Well a woman who'll kiss on the very first date is
usually a hussy
And a woman who'll kiss on the second time out
is anything but fussy
But a woman who'll wait till the third time around
Head in the clouds—Feet on the ground
She's the girl you're glad you found
She's your Shipoopi!
Shipoopi! Shipoopi, Shipoopi

BOYS

The girl who's hard to get!

MARCELLUS

Shipoopi, Shipoopi, Shipoopi

GIRLS

But you can win her yet.

MARCELLUS

Walk her once just to raise the curtain, then you
Walk around twice and make for certain
Once more in the flower garden
She will never get sore if you beg her pardon

ALL

Do re me fa sol la si
Do si la sol fa mi re do

MARCELLUS

Squeeze her once when she isn't lookin', if you
Get a squeeze back, that's fancy cookin'
Once more for a pepper-upper
She will never get sore on her way to supper

ALL

Do re me fa sol la si
Do si do

MARCELLUS

Now little ol' Sal was a No-Gal
As anyone could see
Lookit her now—she's a Go-Gal
Who only goes for me
Squeeze her once when she isn't lookin' if you
Get a squeeze back, that's fancy cookin'
Once more for a pepper-upper
She will never get sore on her way to supper

ALL

Do re me fa sol la si
Do si do

MARCELLUS

Shipoopi, Shipoopi, Shipoopi

BOYS

The girl who's hard to get

MARCELLUS

Shipoopi, Shipoopi, Shipoopi

GIRLS

But you can win her yet
   (*Several* COUPLES *do specialties, including*
   MARCELLUS *and* ETHEL, TOMMY *and* ZANEETA.
   HAROLD *enters.*)

BOY

Come on, Professor, show us some new steps!
   (HAROLD *makes gallant invitation to wall-*
   flower MARIAN. *She is trapped into dancing*
   with him in Vernon Castle one-step. She
   shines. Several of the LADIES *witness this and*
   rush off with the news. The KIDS *all join in*
   again copying the steps HAROLD *and* MARIAN
   are doing.)

ALL

Shipoopi, Shipoopi, Shipoopi
The girl who's hard to get
Shipoopi, Shipoopi, Shipoopi
But you can win her yet

107

You can win her yet!
Shipoopi!
(*As a reprise starts, featuring* TOMMY *and*
ZANEETA, EULALIE *and* MAYOR SHINN *enter.*)

SHINN

Take your hands off my daughter!

ZANEETA

Papa!

TOMMY

Mr. Shinn, your honor. Your daughter and I are goin'
steady behind your back.

SHINN

Why *you—*

TOMMY

We'd rather do it in front a'your back but—

SHINN

Do what? Never mind!

TOMMY

Zaneeta's scared a'ya, but I'm not. I should think you'd
hate to have your own daughter scared a'ya, Jeely Kly.

SHINN

I'm going to warn you once more. If I ever catch you
touching my daughter I'll by God horsewhip you till Hell
won't have it again.

EULALIE

Now, George!
108

SHINN

Not one poop out'a you madam!

EULALIE

(*To* ZANEETA)
I think he means peep.

SHINN

Yes! And now get out'a this public building!

TOMMY

I got as much right in a public building as anybody.

SHINN

Right? How do you get any right around here? Aiding and abetting the swindling activities of this spell-binding cymbal salesman? You know what I see written all over you? Reform School! Now get out! ... Get out, you wild kid!
  (TOMMY *rushes off*)

ZANEETA

Papa, *please*. It's Capulets like you make blood in the market place. Ye Gods.

SHINN

You watch your frazolagy young woman. Go home.
  (ZANEETA *weeps and starts off*. EULALIE *starts after her*)
Eulalie!

EULALIE

Yes, George, I only—

SHINN

You tend to your dance.

EULALIE

(*Coming back*)
My dance—
(SHINN *points, she exits*)

SHINN

I'll handle Zaneeta. Takin' up with wild kids from the wrong side a'town—

MARIAN

Mr. Mayor, if I could just make you understand—

SHINN

Well ya can't And by the way thanks for nothin'. I've read that book you gave me from cover to cover for a whole week now and didn't find a thing!

HAROLD

Mr. Mayor, if you please—

SHINN

I'll settle your hash as soon as I get these premises offa' my oldest girl—
(*He starts off, turns back*)
Yes!

HAROLD

All right but in the meantime I want you to know I'm vouching for Tommy Djilas. That boy's got the confidence of every kid in town—you'll be standing in line waiting to shake his hand by time our Band plays its first concert.

SHINN

By time your band plays its first concert the individual members'll have to foregather in wheel chairs on account of the broken legs they'll get from tripping over their beards. I'll tell you something, my fine young feathered—my feathered young—never mind! Oliver—Jacey—Ewart—Olin!
(THE MEN *quickly attend*)
I want this man's references and I want 'em tonight! Don't let him out'a your sight! He's slipprier'n a Mississippi sturgeon!

OLIVER

Do you mean you want us to get his credentials?

SHINN

Get his papers or get him in jail! Couldn't make myself any clearer if I'se a button hook in the well-water.
(HE *exits, dragging* ZANEETA. *The men follow*)

MARIAN

(*Hurrying to* HAROLD)
Professor Hill I think Mayor Shinn has behaved abominably and I think it was wonderful of you coming to Tommy's defense.

HAROLD

Oh that was nothing.

MARIAN

Yes it was.

HAROLD

Oh no. A man can't dodge the issue every time a little personal risk is involved—
(*Watching her*)

What does the poet say? The coward dies a thousand deaths
—the brave man—only 500.
    (HE *laughs gaily, suddenly turns serious*)
Unfortunately, of course the Mayor was already pretty mad
on account of his Billiard Parlor. *Now—*
    (HE *shrugs ruefully*)
oh, I suppose a recommendation from a musical authority
like yourself would help but—
    (*Leaving*)
I couldn't think of asking you to do a thing like that.

MARIAN

    (*Stopping him*)
Why Professor Hill—

HAROLD

You would?

MARIAN

I'd be glad to. I just wish I was a little more informed—I've
been wanting to talk to you about Winthrop's cornet.

HAROLD

His cornet? Mother-of-pearl keys—

MARIAN

I'm sure it's fine. But you see he never touches it. Oh, the
first week or so, he made a few—ah—experimental—blats? I
guess you'd say?

HAROLD

Yes—yes, blats,

112

MARIAN

And he sings the
> (*Singing it*)

"Minuet in G de da" almost constantly.

HAROLD

> (*Going to the groups of Ladies and leading them as they sing*)

La de da de da de da de da. La de da La de da—

MARIAN

But he never touches the cornet.

HAROLD

Well, you see—

MARIAN

He says you told him it wasn't necessary

HAROLD

Well.

MARIAN

He tells me about some "Think System." If he *thinks* the "Minuet in G" he won't have to bother with notes. Now professor—

HAROLD

Miss Marian. The Think System is a revolutionary method, I'll admit. So was Galileo's conception of the Heavens, Columbus' conception of the egg—ah—globe, Bach's conception of the Well-tempered Clavichord. Hmm? Now I cannot discuss these things here in public.
> (*Spotting the* LADIES *who are entering, he backs off*)

When may I call?

THE MUSIC MAN

Why any night this week—

(THE LADIES *enter as* HAROLD *exits hastily*)

LADIES
Pickalittletalkalittlepickalittletalkalittle
Cheepcheepcheep talkalot
    pickalittlemore
Pickalittletalkalittlepickalittletalkalittle
Cheepcheepcheep talkalot
    pickalittlemore
Pickalittletalkalittlepickalittletalkalittle
Cheepcheepcheeptalkalotpickalittlemore
Pickalittletalkalittlepickalittletalkalittle
Cheepcheepcheepcheepcheepcheep
    cheepcheep.

ETHEL
Miss Paroo, please
join our Del Sarte
Committee.

ALMA
You were so dear
tonight   dancing
The Shipoopi with
Professor Hill.

ALMA
You danced like a
        Fairy princess
        (Slam) (Slam) With a
        Moonbeam for your
        Floor. You had a
        Golden shimmer in your
        Hair and silver
        Shoes for all to
        See (Slam) We
        Know that you will soon unfold a for-
        Giving heart of purest gold
        Here (Thump) where a
        Woman's Heart should
        Be!

ALMA, MAUD, ETHEL, MRS. SQUIRES

Fairy Princess
Moonbeam floor
Golden shimmer
Silver shoes
Now unfold
Heart of gold
Here (Thump) where a
Woman's heart should
Be!

The
Professor told us to
Read those books and we
Simply adored them
All!

ALMA

Chaucer!

ETHEL

Rabelais!

EULALIE

(*Crossing*)
Bal-zac!

LADIES

Cheep,cheep,cheep,cheep,cheep,cheep,cheep,cheep
Cheep,cheep,cheep,cheep,cheep,cheep,cheep,cheep
Cheep,cheep,cheep,cheep,cheep,cheep,cheep,cheep
Pickalittletalkalittle CH!

BLACKOUT

Scene 2

TIME: *The following Wednesday evening. After supper.*

AT RISE: *The Hotel Porch.* JACEY, OLIN, OLIVER, EWART, *all wearing silver stars, are on the alert as* HAROLD *is trying to escape them.*

EWART
Sorry, Professor, but we got our orders.

OLIVER
We all been deputized.

HAROLD
Yes—congratulations. Let's see now—you know all week I've tried to give you fellows my references and credentials but every time you seem to get off the subject somehow. Now I have just what you want up in my hotel room—take me a second.

EWART
Sorry. 'Fraid I'll have to go with you.

HAROLD
Yes—well, let's see if I have my key—
    (*Finds paper in pocket*)
What's this?—Oh—a testimonial from the only female bassoon player ever to appear on the Redpath Circuit, Madame
116

Rini. Her stage name, of course. Actually she was from Moline. Lida Rose Quackenbush.

EWART

(*Reaching*)
Could I just see that for a minute?

HAROLD

(*Hastily pocketing it*)
Oh you'll never forget the name. Lida Rose. Same as the old song.
(*Gets out pitch pipe and blows it*)
(*Sings*)
> Lida Rose, I'm home again, Rose

QUARTET

(*Instantly jumping in*)
> To get the sun back in my sky
> Lida Rose, I'm home again, Rose
> About a thousand kisses shy
> Ding dong ding
> I can hear the chapel bell chime
> Ding dong ding
> At the least suggestion
> I'll pop the question
> Lida Rose, I'm home again, Rose
> Without a sweetheart to my name
> Lida Rose, now everyone knows

(*As the* QUARTET *starts,* HAROLD *dusts off his hands, leaves the porch and joins* MARCELLUS *who has entered Left and is beckoning to* HAROLD. *They exit Left hastily.*)

That I am hoping you're the
    same
So here is my love song
Not fancy or fine
Lida Rose, oh won't you be mine
Lida Rose oh Lida Rose oh Lida Rose oh

        (*Lights fade out on* QUARTET *as Paroo Porch
        swings into view Stage Left*)
    (MARIAN *is sitting on the porch steps,* MRS. PAROO *in
rocker on porch*)

                MARIAN
    (*Sings*)
    Dream of now
    Dream of then
    Dream of a love song
    That might have been.
    Do I love you?
    Oh yes, I love you
    And I'll bravely tell you
    But only when
    We dream again
    Sweet and low, Sweet and low,
    How sweet that mem'ry
    How long ago
    Forever?
    Oh yes, forever
    Will I ever tell you?
    Ah—no.
        (*Lights come up on* QUARTET)
        (MARIAN *and* QUARTET *sing together.*)

MARIAN	QUARTET
Dream of now	Lida Rose, I'm home again, Rose
Dream of then	To get the sun back in my sky
Dream of a love song	Lida Rose, I'm home again, Rose
That might have been	About a thousand kisses shy.
Do I love you?	Ding dong ding
Oh yes, I love you	I can hear the chapel bell chime
And I'll bravely tell you	Ding dong ding
But only when	At the least suggestion
We dream again	I'll pop the question
Sweet and low, Sweet and low	Lida Rose, I'm home again, Rose
How sweet that mem'ry	Without a sweetheart to my name.
How long ago	Lida Rose, now everyone knows
Forever?	That I am hoping you're the same
Oh yes, forever	So here is my love song
Will I ever tell you?	Not fancy or fine
Ah—no.	Lida Rose, oh won't you be mine.
	Lida Rose oh Lida Rose oh Lida Rose

(*Lights fade out on* QUARTET)

Scene 3

TIME: *Immediately following*

The Paroo Porch. MARIAN *is sitting on the steps in the moonlight.* MRS. PAROO *is rocking and sewing.*

MRS. PAROO
(*Testily*)
Will you ever stop arguin' with yourself? "Will you ever tell him—won't you ever tell him—ah yes—ah no"—ah fiddlesticks. Just open your mouth and let it come out.

MARIAN
Now Mama—

MRS. PAROO
Now nuthin'. If he ever comes to call again, you see him alone, and if you haven't the gumption to tell him how you feel—

MARIAN
Tell him?

MRS. PAROO
Well, there's nothing wrong with a ladylike hint.

WINTHROP
(*Bursting in with a jar of worms*)
Mama!

120

MRS. PAROO

Winthrop, where've you been?

WINTHROP

Fithin'.

MRS. PAROO

Fishing!

WINTHROP

With Harold.

MARIAN

You mean Professor Hill?

WINTHROP

Mm hm. And look I thtill have some wormth left.

MARIAN

Did you have a good time?

WINTHROP

Thcrumpthyuth. He told me all about hith home town,
Gary Indiana. And he thaid he'd take me there thum day.
And he taught me a thong that hardly hath any etheth in it.
(*He hands* MARIAN *the worms.*)
(*Sings*)

Gary Indiana, Gary Indiana, Gary Indiana
Let me thay it wunth again
Gary Indiana, Gary Indiana, Gary Indiana
That'th the town that "knew me when"
If you'd like to have a logical ekthplanathyun
How I happened on thith elegant thinkopathyun
I will thay without a moment of hethitathyun

121

There ith jutht one plathe
That can light my fathe
Gary Indiana
Gary Indiana
Not Loueetheeana, Parith Franth, New York or
        Rome, but
Gary Indiana
Gary Indiana
Gary Indiana
My home thweet home
If you'd like to have a logical ekthplanathyun
How I happened on thith elegant thinkopathyun
I will thay without a moment of hethitathyun
There ith jutht one plathe
That can light my fathe

MRS. PAROO

Gary Indiana

MARIAN

Gary Indiana

WINTHROP

Not Loueetheeana, Parith Franth, New York or
    Rome, but—

MRS. PAROO

Gary Indiana

MARIAN

Gary Indiana

ALL THREE

Gary Indiana

My home sweet home.
> (WINTHROP *does a quick dance step on the*
> *tag.*)

WINTHROP
(Grabs his worms and runs into house, reappears im-
mediately)
I'll be back in a minute. I have to thow Amaryllith my live
frog.
> (*He runs off singing the "Minuet in G"*)
La de da de da de da de da. La de da. La de da.
> (MRS. PAROO *starts into the house*)

MARIAN
Leave the dishes—I'll do them, Mama.

MRS. PAROO
Don't you have to change for the sociable?

MARIAN
There's time later.
> (CHARLIE COWELL *enters left, passes porch, turns back*)

CHARLIE
Shinns live around here somewhere?

MARIAN
The Shinn home is on East Elm. This is West Elm.

CHARLIE
Aw Criminee!
> (HE *sees "PIANO GIVEN" sign on porch*)
I see you're the piano teacher in town? You must know
about this fellow Hill formin' a boys' band here.

MARIAN

Yes.

CHARLIE

Well, don't let it worry you no more. I got the goods on him in spades. Swindlin' two-bit thimble rigger. That's why I got to see Shinn.
(*Pulls out watch*)
I'm just passin' through. Number eight only makes a fifteen minute water stop. Wish it was twenty. Could sure concentrate five minutes on you, girly-girl.

MARIAN

Who are you?
(SHE *rises*)

CHARLIE

Name's Charlie Cowell—anvil salesman. But just now I'm out to protect the good name of the travellin' fraternity from this swindler.

MARIAN

Mr. Cowell, you're making a big mistake.

CHARLIE

Mistake my old lady's corset-cover! That fella's been the raspberry seed in my wisdom tooth just long enough. He spoiled Illinois for me and he's not gonna spoil Iowa! Say, what kind of music teacher are you you didn't see through him? He's no more Professor—

MARIAN

I know all about that. Band leaders are always called Professor. It's a harmless deception. He's a fine director and his scholastic—

124

CHARLIE

Fine director? Now wait a minute—Have you heard one
note a' music from any band?

MARIAN

No, but—

CHARLIE

But nothin', girly-girl! He never formed a band in his life!
And he never will!

MARIAN

If you'll just listen to me for a minute—

CHARLIE

I'd like to—I'd like to do more than that, if I had the time.
I sure got the inclination. But I got to get back on that train
and I got to leave this dynamite
    (*Brandishing papers*)
with *some*body on the way't the deppo. 'By, girly-girl. See
you next time through.
    (*Train whistle is heard*)

MARIAN

You'll never make that train at the depot. You'll have to
catch it at the crossing.
    (*She gestures Left*)

CHARLIE

No *sir*. I've got to leave word. And I can see you ain't the
one to leave it with.

MARIAN

Just a minute Mr. Cowell—you—don't know me yet.

125

CHARLIE

(*Turning back*)
Is that an invitation?

MARIAN

(*Losing her nerve*)
No—I meant I don't know *you*, and—

CHARLIE

(*Turning away again*)
Yes—I'd need more time anyway—

MARIAN

I mean as well as I'd like to—

CHARLIE

(*Turning back*)
No trouble *there*, girly-girl.
(*He moves in*)

MARIAN

(*Drawing back*)
I never met a man who sells anvils. That's something—well—
quite different.

CHARLIE

(*Pawing a little*)
Takes a salesman, I can tell you that. Anvils have a limited
appeal you know.
(*Train whistle*)
What am I *doin'*? I miss that train I'll get fired! And I got
to leave word about that fellow Hill!

MARIAN

Leave word with me.

126

CHARLIE

Not on your tintype. How do I know you'd deliver these letters?

MARIAN

Try me.
(*Grabbing his lapels, she plants her lips on his. It is a long kiss. The train grows louder... We hear off-stage the* QUARTET *singing "Lida Rose." She struggles free, wipes her mouth in disgust, points L.*)
There's your train! Now run for it!

CHARLIE

(*Furious*)
Why you double-dealing little— Who do you think you're protecting? That guy's got a girl in every county in Illinois, and he's taken it away from every one of 'em! And that's 102 counties! Not counting the piana teachers like you he cozies up to, to keep their mouths shut!
(*As he runs off*)
Neither one of you's heard the last of me, girly-girl!
(MARIAN *stands stunned.* QUARTET *enters singing and stops long enough for*)

QUARTET

Good evening, Miss Marian.
(MARIAN *still stands dazed, not even acknowledging their presence. They exit singing.* MRS. PAROO *is heard offstage*)

MRS. PAROO

(*Off*)
Marian... Marian!
(*She comes out on the Porch*)

127

Marian dear! Who was you talkin' to just—
(HAROLD *enters*)
Why Professor Hill!

HAROLD

Mrs. Paroo! The top a' the evening! Miss Marian.

MRS. PAROO

You and Marian come up and set. I—I've—I've got some jelly on the stove.

MARIAN

There's no jelly on the stove, Mama.

MRS. PAROO

(*Tartly—exiting*)
Well, I'll put some on.
(MARIAN *stands mute*)

HAROLD

(*After a pause*)
Shall we "set" as your mother said?

MARIAN

Well, I..

HAROLD

You did ask me to call ...?

MARIAN

Did I? ... I didn't mean anything ...
128

HAROLD

Now Miss Marian, I'm not suggesting your invitation inferred anything but academic enlightenment.
   (SHE *looks at him quizzically*)
The Think System? I've been by your house to try to explain it to you a time or two this week but there always seemed to be people around—mostly ladies I thought.

MARIAN

Yes, Mrs. Squires and several of the ladies.

HAROLD

I'm glad—wouldn't want anybody beating my time.
   (*Laughs*) (*Long pause*)
You wouldn't? No ma'am...Well, it's evidently not the convenient night. See you at the sociable later.
   (*He starts to leave*)

MARIAN

Professor Hill...Is it true that you've—
   (*She starts to lose her nerve*)
had a hundred...what I'm trying to say is...

HAROLD

   (*Advancing to her*)
Yes?

MARIAN

   (*Completely losing her nerve*)
Is it really true that you've developed a...a Think System?

HAROLD

A what? A Think System? Oh—Think System—yes. It's really very simple. As simple as whistling. Nobody has to

show you how to use your lips in whistling. You only have
to think a tune to have it come out clearly here.
(*Pointing to her lips*)
Now just try this yourself, before you ask any questions.
(*He puckers up*)

MARIAN

(*Pulling back*)
I take your word.

HAROLD

Could we sit down?

MARIAN

Are all music teachers as dense as I am?

HAROLD

All music teachers?

MARIAN

I daresay you meet dozens—even a hundred—

HAROLD

Well I—

MARIAN

(*Cutting in*)
Have they all been as fascinated as I have with . . . the Think
System?

HAROLD

Some more, some less. One young lady had thought up the
same system before I got to her town. She showed me a few
refinements . . .

MARIAN
(*Turning away*)
I see...

HAROLD
Have I said something wrong?

MARIAN
(*Turned away from him*)
Please don't let me keep you, Professor Hill. You must have many more important things to do than to explain the Think System to me.

HAROLD
Can't think of a one.

MARIAN
And I must be very dull company for a man of your experience.

HAROLD
Now saaaay ... where'd you get an idea like that?

MARIAN
One hears rumors of travelling salesmen.

HAROLD
Now, Miss Marian—you mustn't believe everything you hear. After all, one even hears rumors about librarians.

MARIAN
(*Turning on him*)
I suppose you're referring to Uncle Maddy.

HAROLD

Uncle Maddy?

MARIAN

Mr. Madison—my father's best friend. No matter what they say he left me that library job so Mother and Winthrop and I would have some security. Surely you don't believe...

HAROLD

Of course not! That's exactly what I'm saying. But why do you think people start those rumors.

MARIAN

Narrow-mindedness, jealousy—jealousy, mostly, I guess.

HAROLD

Exactly. And jealousy mostly starts rumors about travelling salesmen.
(*Catching her off-guard. Quietly*)
What have you heard?

MARIAN

Oh—oh nothing about you personally—just generally—

HAROLD

What have you heard generally?

MARIAN

Just that—
(*He is very close to her*)
but of course, it stands to reason that—that disappointment and jealousy can lead to—I mean—take you for instance—

132

your attentions to—to—customers and—and well, teachers
might easily be misinterpreted mightn't they ...
   (*Frantically hoping for reassurance*)
I mean, now honestly—mightn't they?

HAROLD

Why ..

MARIAN

   (*Racing on*)
And, as you say—if another salesman—or somebody were
jealous—I mean—well, they could be downright lies—
couldn't they?

HAROLD

   (*Confused*)
What could?

MARIAN

Rumors and things.

HAROLD

Why, of course.

MARIAN

It just proves you should never believe everything you hear,
doesn't it? I mean if you discuss things ...

HAROLD

Miss Marian, I would be delighted to discuss anything in
the world with you. But couldn't we do it sitting down?
   (*Trying to lighten her mood*)
You do sit? ... Your knees bend and all.

MARIAN

We could sit on the porch steps.

HAROLD

We could also sit on a large hollow log over't the footbridge.

MARIAN

I couldn't think of it. I've never been to the footbridge with a man in my life.

HAROLD

Just to talk.

MARIAN

I've got to dress for the sociable.

HAROLD

Then meet me there in fifteen minutes.

MARIAN

I just can't—please—some other time—maybe tomorrow.

HAROLD

My dear little librarian— Pile up enough tomorrows and you'll find you've collected nothing but a lot of empty yesterdays. I don't know about you but I'd like to make today worth remembering.

MARIAN

(*Breathlessly*)
Oh—so would I.

HAROLD

The footbridge—fifteen minutes.

MARIAN

Fifteen minutes.
>   (HAROLD *exits quickly*. MARIAN's *voice is suddenly loud
>   and desperate*)
Mama!

MRS. PAROO

>   (*Coming onto porch*)
What?

MARIAN

I just told Professor Hill I'd meet him at the footbridge in
fifteen minutes.

MRS. PAROO

Glory be and the saints be praised it works!

MARIAN

What does?

MRS. PAROO

I been usin' the Think System on you from the parlor!

BLACKOUT

Scene 4

TIME: *Fifteen minutes later*

AT RISE: The Footbridge. The Stage is dark. As the traveller opens we see Townspeople crossing the Bridge on their way to the sociable, the QUARTET *in Indian regalia, the* LADIES *in their Grecian Draperies, and everybody dressed in their best carrying picnic baskets, freezers, etc. The Lights iris up to reveal all the teen-age couples in romantic poses. They dance to a waltz tempo version of "It's You" as the last young lady escapes her escort and runs off R.* HAROLD *reappears, looks for* MARIAN, *then raps on the bridge with a large twig he is carrying. He conducts with the twig as though he were leading an orchestra. He catches himself, breaks the twig and throws it away.*

MARCELLUS
(*Entering in a rush*)
Hey Greg! The uniforms have arrived! The kids are in 'em already. The people are going to be screaming for music if those kids show up at the Sociable.

HAROLD
Yeah—

MARCELLUS

(*Handing* HAROLD *a roll*)

Here's most a' the dough. I got Tommy to collect it. He's trying to keep the kids together at least. Pretending to hold a practice over't the lumber yard.

HAROLD

All right, Marce. Get the rig.

MARCELLUS

I got it!

HAROLD

What time's the freight go?

MARCELLUS

Nine-forty from the junction.

HAROLD

Well it's not even eight thirty yet—

MARCELLUS

Look, you wanta turtle-wurtle around here and get yourself caught in a bunny-trap, you go ahead, but—

HAROLD

Don't worry, Marce. I'll meet you at the Hotel in plenty a'time.

(MARCELLUS *exits as* MARIAN *enters*)

HAROLD

Miss Marian!

(*They rush toward each other and meet on the bridge*)

You're late.

MARIAN

But you said fifteen minutes—

HAROLD

I meant that you were about—well I'd say—about twenty-six years late—took you all this time to get to the footbridge with a fella.

MARIAN

If you want to know the truth it was almost longer.

HAROLD

Oh?

MARIAN

Halfway here I nearly turned back. I suppose I'm not the first person to find it easier to think clearly when not under the spell of your salesmanship.

HAROLD
(*Protesting too much*)
Now Miss Marian—surely you don't think I've been selling *you* anything.

MARIAN

No—you've given me something. That's why I decided to come.

HAROLD
(*Bewildered*)
I don't recall giving—
(MUSIC *under following*)
138

MARIAN

(*With intensity*)

Oh yes, you have! Something beautiful. That's why I came
—and I'm glad! Oh, please don't be afraid that I expect too
much more. One can't expect a *travelling* salesman to stay
put. I know there have been many ports of call—and there
will be many more. But that's no reason for me not to be
grateful for what you will have left behind for *me!*

HAROLD

(*Beginning to protest*)

Marian—I—

MARIAN

(*Raising hand to silence him, she sings*)

There were bells on the hill but I never heard them
ringing
No, I never heard them at all
Till there was you
There were birds in the sky but I never saw them
winging
No I never saw them at all
Till there was you
And there was music, and there were wonderful
roses, they tell me,
In sweet fragrant meadows of dawn and dew.
There was love all around but I never heard it
singing
No, I never heard it at all
Till there was you
(*Orchestra boils up and over in eight bar
extension as they kiss*)

HAROLD & MARIAN

There was love all around but I never heard it
    singing
No, I never heard it at all
Till there was you.
    (*They kiss again as* MARCELLUS *appears*)

HAROLD

Marian, there's a lot of things you don't know about me—

MARCELLUS

    (*Whispering loudly*)
Psssst! Hey Greg!

HAROLD

Excuse me. I'm expecting a cable from Hector Berlioz—
this could be it.
    (*He hurries to meet* MARCELLUS)
Now what?

MARCELLUS

Who's the salesman here? Sounds like she's selling and
you're buying.

HAROLD

You nuts? I didn't know I'se goin' to be able to leave
tonight—I had to keep her off balance, didn't I? I told you—

MARCELLUS

Well, she's so far off balance now you can't tell her from a
cat-boat in a hurricane.

HAROLD

Listen, Buster Brown, I've come up through the ranks on this skirmish and I'm not resigning without my commission.

MARCELLUS

But Greg—you can't get anywhere right out here on the footbridge.

HAROLD

There's a place over't Madison Park near the sociable makes this footbridge look like the old ladies home. Now beat it. Go get the rig.
(MARCELLUS *exits as* HAROLD *returns to* MARIAN)
Never a peaceful moment in the music business.
(*Preparing for the kill*)
Now then where were we?

MARIAN

You were about to tell me what I don't know about you.

HAROLD

Yeah—well we really don't have to go into that just now, do we?

MARIAN

No we don't—or ever for that matter, Harold. The librarian hasn't felt much like doing research lately—but she did plenty when you first came here.

HAROLD

(*Slightly apprehensive*)
Oh—about what?

MARIAN

Oh—about Professor Harold Hill, Gary Conservatory of Music—Gold Medal Class of '05. Harold, there wasn't any Gary Conservatory in '05.

HAROLD

Why there certainly—

MARIAN

Because the town wasn't even built till '06.
    (*She kisses him, and starts off*)
I'll see you at the sociable.

HAROLD

    (*Calling after her*)
You knew all the time?!

MARIAN

    (*Returning, she takes out a paper*)
Since July 7th—three days after you came. I tore this page out of the Indiana Journal.
    (*She hands it to him*)
It was originally intended to use against you but now I give it to you with all my heart.

HAROLD

But if you knew—why didn't you—
    (MARIAN *throws him another kiss as she exits*)
Why you little—
    (HAROLD *preens himself as he thinks all this over—enjoying his prowess and his luck—he starts off right as traveller closes in.*)

Scene 5

TIME: *Immediately following.*

AT RISE: HAROLD *before traveller.*

         HAROLD
      (*Whistles first phrase*)
      (*Sings*)
While 110 cornets played the air
Then I modestly took my place
As the one and only bass
And I oom-pahed up and down the square.

         MARIAN'S VOICE
      (*Offstage*)
Goodnight my someone, goodnight my love

         HAROLD
With a hundred and ten cornets right behind

         MARIAN'S VOICE
      (*Offstage*)
Our star is shining its brightest light

         HAROLD
      (*Taking paper re Gary from his pocket*)
There were horns of every shape and kind—
        (HAROLD *recoils in a gigantic delayed take—*

143

*struck by lightning—as the realization hits him
that he is in love)*
Sweet dreams be yours, dear
If dreams there be.

MARIAN'S VOICE
(Offstage)
While a hundred and ten cornets played the air—

HAROLD
I wish I may and I wish I might.
Now goodnight my someone, goodnight.

MARCELLUS
(Entering with HAROLD's *suitcase in one hand, desperately holding off* COWELL *with the other)*
Greg, this guy's crazy. He's goin' all over town spillin' everything.

COWELL
(Screaming mad)
I'll say I'm crazy! Missed my train—prob'ly lost my job! But I got ya now, Hill, and you'll pay! You'd be in the clink right now had'na been fer that piana teacher. I told her all about you and wha'd she do? Lolligags me around till I couldn't get to Shinn! Little dried up man-hungry doxy, round-heel fiz gig—
*(*HAROLD *knocks* CHARLIE *down)*

HAROLD
Get outa here or I'll kill you, you dirty-mouthed—
144

COWELL

(*Scrambling off*)
You bully! I'll stay in this town till you get yours up, down, through and sideways! You big blow-off! Why you never even knew the territory!

MARCELLUS

Here's your stuff, Greg! The rig's in the alley—Come on! Hurry up!
(MARCELLUS *exits with suitcase, as* HAROLD *stands—not moving*)

CURTAIN

Scene 6

TIME: *A few minutes later.*

AT RISE: Madison Park. The Ice Cream Sociable. The last strains of "Rustle of Spring" are heard as the LADIES *are concluding their Grecian Urn presentation.*

EULALIE

Two Grecian Urns! And a fountain—
>   (*There is mild applause.* CHARLIE COWELL & MAYOR
>   SHINN *burst in among the* LADIES)

SHINN

Stop, stop. Listen to this man!

CHARLIE

You gullible green-grass goats! Can't you get it through your heads that you're being swindled out'a your eye teeth right now—this minute? There's a burglar in the bedroom while you're fiddling in the parlor! I'm talking about Harold Hill—road agent—highwayman—pickpocket.

MAN #1

Pickpocket?

CHARLIE

Same thing! He's had his hand in your wallet, Mister, and yours, Madam, and yours, little lady, ever since the first

146

moment he came to this town! There's more documented evidence here than you'll ever have time to read! There *isn't* any band, there never *has been* any band and there never *will be* any band! And if you don't hunt this man down right now like a mad dog, there won't be any Harold Hill either! He'll be on the next train out of town.

SHINN

Now will you believe me?

MAN #2

Well what are we waiting for?

WOMAN

I want my money back!

MAN #1

Money back—I want his hide!

SHINN

After him! And when you find him bring him to the schoolhouse. After him!
(*He dispatches various groups*)
Try the low road! Look by the crick! Try the mill! Back a'the privy!
(*The* PEOPLE *all rush off. The traveller closes. We see* WINTHROP *alone in front of the traveller. 3 boys cross R to L. The* GRECIAN LADIES *cross from L to R behind traveller.* WINTHROP *breaks down and runs off L weeping.* MARIAN *rushes across from R to L. Two* GROUPS *cross each other behind traveller, one group going L, one group going R.* HAROLD & MARCELLUS *rush across from L to R in front of the traveller. Another* GROUP *including the* QUARTET *rushes across*

147

after him, L to R, in front of the traveller. HAROLD &
MARCELLUS *reappear crossing from R to L in front of
the traveller as* MARIAN *crosses from L to R in front
of the traveller. They pass each other.* HAROLD *stops
abruptly, and calls her.*)

HAROLD

Marian! I've been looking all over for you! Where've
you been?

MARIAN

(Rushing to him)
Harold! I've been looking for Winthrop—he's run away!
Please go! Please, Harold, they're even talking about tar
and feathers!

HAROLD

I had to see you, Marian—

MARIAN

It's all right! Don't you *know* that? You don't owe me a
word—not a word— Please, hurry, *please*—

MARCELLUS

(Rushing to him)
Greg—
    *(Attracted by off-stage activity, desperately calls in
    off-stage direction)*
He isn't anywhere around here! Let's try down by the
crick!
    (He exits and WINTHROP *rushes through looking over
    his shoulder)*

MARIAN

Winthrop!
(Grabbing him)
(WINTHROP *breaks away but* HAROLD *catches him*)

HAROLD

Hey, wait a minute here, son.

WINTHROP

(Struggling)
I'm not your thon! Leave me go!

HAROLD

Not till I talk to you for a minute.

WINTHROP

(Trying to fight loose)
I won't lithen! You wouldn't tell the truth anyway.

HAROLD

I would too.

WINTHROP

Would not.

HAROLD

Would tot! Tell you anything you want to know.

WINTHROP

(Holding still for a minute)
Can you lead a band?

HAROLD

No.

WINTHROP

Are you a big liar?

HAROLD

Yes.

WINTHROP

Are you a dirty rotten crook?

HAROLD

Yes.

WINTHROP

(*Bursting into tears, kicking and squirming*)
Leave me go, you big liar!

HAROLD

What's the matter? You wanted the truth, didn't you? Now I'm bigger'n you and you're going to stand here and get it all so you might as well quit wiggling.
(WINTHROP *finally stops exhausted, stands panting*)
There are two things you're entitled to know. One, you're a wonderful kid. I thought so from the first. That's why I wanted you in the band, so you'd quit mopin' around feeling sorry for yourself!

WINTHROP

(*Sarcastically*)
What band?

HAROLD

... I always think there's a band, kid.

WINTHROP

What'th the other thing I'm entitled to know?

HAROLD

Well—Actually the other thing isn't any of your business now that I think of it.

WINTHROP

I with you'd never come to River Thity!

MARIAN

No you don't, Winthrop.
   ("*Till There Was You*" *in* B.G.)

WINTHROP

Thithter! You *believe* him?

MARIAN

I believe everything he ever said.

WINTHROP

But he promithed uth—

MARIAN

I know what he promised us and it all happened just like he said. The lights. And the flags and the colors. And the cymbals.

WINTHROP

Where wath all that?

MARIAN

   (*Hotly*)
In the way every kid in this town walked around here all summer, and looked and acted. Especially you! And the parents, too. Does Mama wish he'd never come to River City?

151

WINTHROP

Well *you* do, don't you?

MARIAN

No, Winthrop. Now go, Harold—Please.

WINTHROP

(*Bursting into tears*)
Go on, Profethor, hurry up.

HAROLD

I can't go, Winthrop.

WINTHROP

Why not?

HAROLD

For the first time in my life I got my foot caught in the door.

(*Sings to* MARIAN)
There was love all around
But I never heard it singing
No I never heard it at all
Till there was you.
(*They embrace*)

MARCELLUS

(*Entering*)
Greg!
(*Desperately*)
Greg, they're here! That way—that way!

152

WINTHROP

Go on Profethor! That way—that way!

    (HAROLD *stays where he is as the* MEN *surround him.*
    CONSTABLE LOCKE *takes charge with handcuffs*)

CURTAIN

Scene 7

TIME: *Immediately following*

AT RISE: *The scene is River City High School Assembly Room.* TOWNSPEOPLE *assembled. In evidence are the* DEL SARTE LADIES *and the other program participants.*

SHINN

(On the podium)

——which is why I interrupted the program at this point. Rest assured this snake in our bosom would have been misapprehended by this time. Yes! And always remember—

(Gesturing with packet of papers)

fellow River Citizians, I can only remind you that I did everything in my power to prevent this dire happening from—ah—happening. Four score—

MAN #1

What have you done to get our money back?

MAN #2

That Professor collected nearly three hundred dollars for uniforms, just tonight!

WOMAN #1

And we haven't even seen them uniforms yet!

154

SHINN

He's slippery. I *told* you—

WOMAN #2

I haven't seen any uniform or my boy either, since just after
supper!

MAN #3

He's a kidnapper!

WOMAN #3

Fine situation here!

SHINN

Four score—
(CONSTABLE LOCKE *enters and signals to* MAYOR SHINN.
SHINN'S *face takes on a self-satisfied smile*)
Just a minute! Virtue has triumphed! The sword of restibu-
tion has cut down Professor Harold Hill!
(HAROLD *enters in custody*, MARIAN *at his side*. CROWD
reaction. Several of the MEN *rush for* HAROLD. CON-
STABLE *pushes them back*.)
And if there are those, as I have heard, who are melting tar
and collecting feathers, I will not say them nay!

MARIAN
(*Rushing up to the rostrum*)
Well I should think there ought to be some of you who
could forget our everlasting Iowa stubborn chip-on-the-
shoulder arrogance long enough to remember River City
before Harold Hill arrived. Do you remember? Well, *do*
you? Surely some of you ought to be grateful to him for
what he's brought to River City and if so I should think
you'd want to admit it.

155

You're wasting a great deal of time here. If there's a person in this hall who does not think this man Hill should be tarred and feathered, let him stand up.

(*The silence is ear-splitting. Then* MRS. PAROO *stands. Next,* ZANEETA, *then the* SCHOOL BOARD QUARTET, *the* WA TAN YE *girls, the* LADIES OF THE DANCE COMMITTEE, *finally* CONSTABLE LOCKE, *and* EULALIE.)

Eulalie, set down!

(*She sits, but at a gesture from* MRS. PAROO *rises again immediately.*)

And the rest a'you standin' there like a cote a'Shropshyre sheep!

(*They all sit slowly*)

Have you people forgotten how you bought expensive uniforms, technical instruction books and high-priced band instruments? Have you forgotten the clear understanding and warrantee that your children would be taught to play in a band? Well, where's the band? *Where's the band?*

(TOMMY *enters with kids in uniforms too big and too small. He blows whistle. The* KIDS *hold up their instruments in playing position.* HAROLD *stands aghast.* MARIAN *quickly takes a pointer from the blackboard, breaks off a "baton," hands it to* HAROLD.)

(*Looks around desperately, finds no place to hide*)
(*Fervently*)

Think, men, think!

(*He gives the upbeat and leads the* BAND *in "Minuet in G" as it has never been played before—just barely recognizable. The River Citizens think it's the greatest thing they ever heard.* SHINN *crosses to* TOMMY *in amazement—shakes hands with him*)

ALMA

That's my Barney! That tuba's my Barney!

MAN #1

Eddie! That's Eddie's clarionette!

MAUD

Linus, play to me son, play to me!

MAN #2

Davey, my Davey.

SHINN

(*At cornet solo*)
Mrs. Paroo, that's Winthrop!
(MRS. PAROO *registers thrills and pride*)
(HAROLD *has been standing taller with each exclamation, and now conducts with a flourish; the same inimitable* HAROLD HILL *of before.* SHINN *crosses, shakes his hand.* PEOPLE *cheer.* COWELL *exits.* HAROLD *embraces* MARIAN.)

CURTAIN

END OF PLAY